Sunspot Literary Journal

2024

Creativity is Power

Sunspot Literary Journal 2024
Volume 6 Issue 4
Creativity is Power

Published by Sun Dogs Creations
Changing the World One Book at a Time
Print ISBN: 978-1-951389-37-6
eBook ISBN: 978-1-951389-38-3

Cover Image *Galaxy Room* by Emily Dolanová
Cover Design by Angel Leya
Sunspot Logo by Timothy Boardman

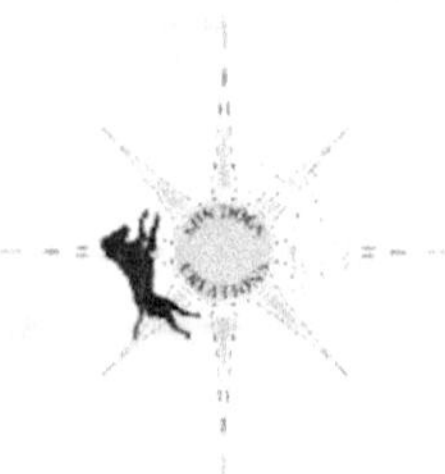

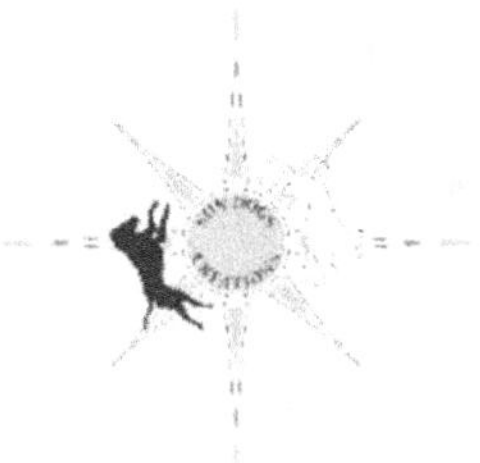

TABLE OF CONTENTS

Solar Flare 2024

AI and Creativity

A Peep at the Moon / Tianyagenv Yan

NIGHTMARE / TIANYAGENV YAN

Yet You

Jane Wiseman

anything they said was said slap on it
but what you said came out of the red deep

had a nostril big as a person could sit in it
feet like the sailing off the golden sheen

anything they did they did like one two three
but yours was a silver purse for fishes and fronds

you hauled it up the holy bronze of the deck
across the boards you spilled for only me

the dreams they dreamed were small and gray
dreams of yours towered to thunderheads

drifting the continent oh I could feel
the lightning flash from the dark underside
and the leading boil of it sang shrill and green

Waiting Out the Storm / Robin Young

AM3 / Anita Maksimiuk

The Melon Stand

Jackson Mills Smith

The Melon Stand
    is a horsefly catch-all,
    a deerfly junction.

One's got to be as quick as a rabbit hound
to drop a dollar in the Ball jar.

I prefer thieving one or two from the acres
to take my time in choosing,
traipsing between the bee boxes and loader buses
after parking in the cover of chokecherry.

This way I can knuckle knock each one
and find the sweetest to share.

If a quad rolls up to bust me
I tell the driver I've got a sister
about to marry a melon man, whose family plots
go back to the treaty lines.

Show me an act of theft that doesn't call for patience.
Show me a wealth that's come to anyone honestly.

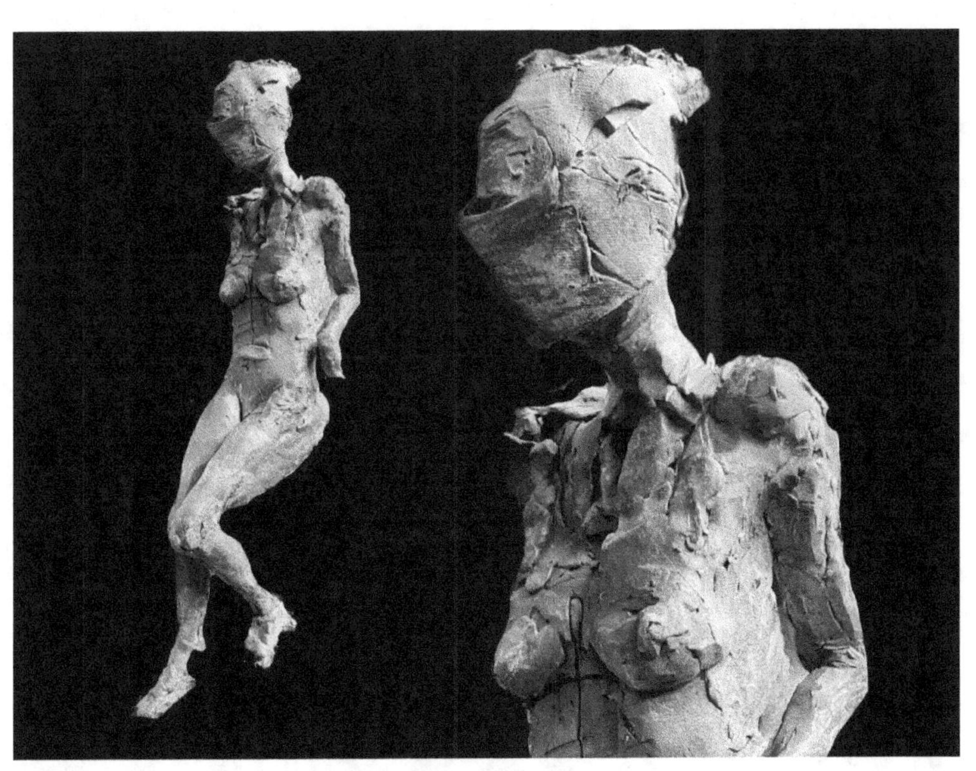

THE VEIL / ALEKSANDRA SCEPANOVIC

Incomprehensible: What AI Could Not / Aimee Bungard

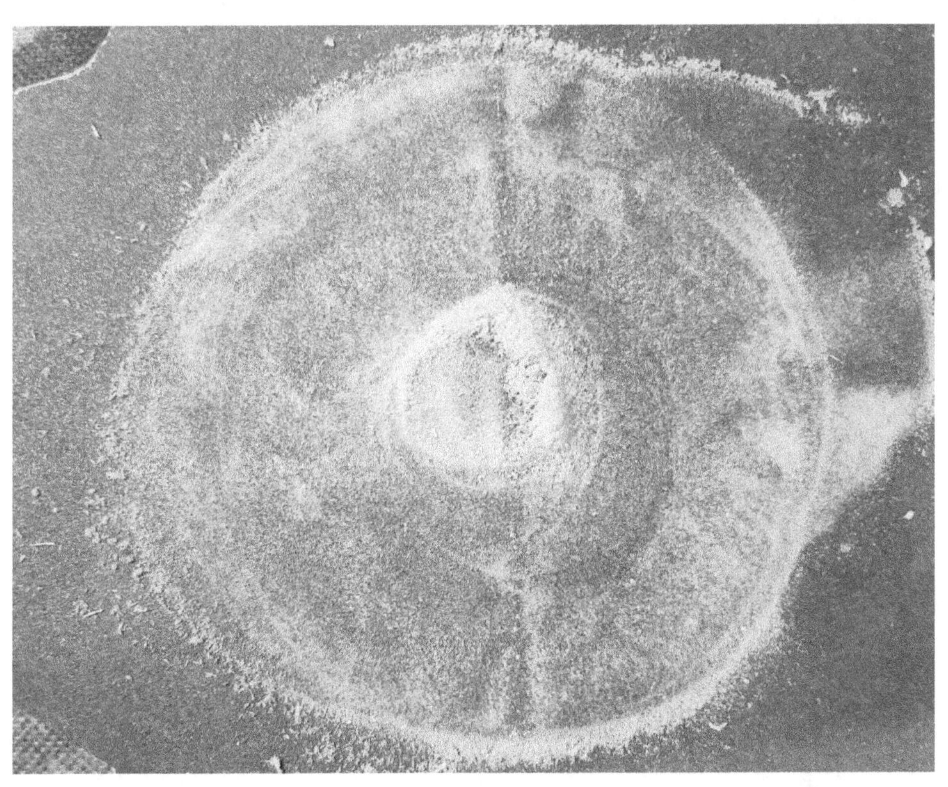

Anomalous Introspection

/ Robert Gillespie

Ode to Your Hands

Pablo Neruda

Translated from Spanish by Wally Swist

When your hands reach out,
love, into mine,
what do they bring me flying?
why did they stop
in my mouth, suddenly?
why do I recognize them,
as if then, before,
I would have touched them
as if before their being
they would have traveled
to my forehead, my waist?

Their softness came
flying over time,
over the sea, over smoke,
about spring,
and when you placed
your hands on my chest,
I recognized those wings,
golden dove, in them
I perceived that clay
and that color of wheat.

The years of my life
I walked looking for them.
I climbed the stairs,
I crossed the reefs,
trains dispatched me,
the waters delivered me,
and in the skin of the grapes
I thought I touched you,
the wood all at once
brought me your contact,
the almond announced to me
your secret softness,
until your hands
closed on my chest
and there like two wings
they finished their journey.

Oda a tus Manos

Pablo Neruda

Cuando tus manos salen,
amor, hacia las mías,
qué me traen volando?
Por qué se detuvieron
en mi boca, de pronto,
por qué las reconozco
como si entonces, antes,
las hubiera tocado,
como si antes de ser
hubieran recorrido
mi frente, mi cintura?

Su suavidad venía
volando sobre el tiempo,
sobre el mar, sobre el humo,
sobre la primavera,
y cuando tú pusiste
tus manos en mi pecho,
reconocí esas alas
de paloma dorada,
reconocí esa greda
y ese color de trigo.

Los años de mi vida
yo caminé buscándolas.

Subí las escaleras,
crucé los arrecifes,
me llevaron los trenes,
las aguas me trajeron,
y en la piel de las uvas
me pareció tocarte.
La madera de pronto
me trajo tu contacto,
la almendra me anunciaba
tu suavidad secreta,
hasta que se cerraron
tus manos en mi pecho
y allí como dos alas
terminaron su viaje.

GRAND HIGHWAY / GJ GILLESPIE

FERRY LANDING 2 / LESLIE KERBY

Regarding Ladders

Joannie Stangeland

That the ladder leans against the north wall
all winter, the ladder counting on the wall.
That I do not trust the ladder.
That in dreams, the top rungs
go missing, a gap to reach across.
That weather gusts and blusters from the south,
the ladder on the leeward side if our house
is the vessel to harbor us
through a marriage long enough
that a new roof is needed while leaves clot
the gutters, the ceaseless rain
streaming over.
                                        That a task, half started,
might wait until spring. That you ask me
to stand at the bottom, to hold
steady the rails. That when you ascend,
my heart will tilt inside my throat,
that ladder in my mind extending
what we have repaired, what we keep undone.

Mysterious Classical Monument

/ Michael Noonan

DECORATED VASE / MICHAEL NOONAN

Chicken Man

Ronnie Yates

Editor's Prize

The Chicken Man has dusky arms and the head of a warrior. Shaved head but for on top, that blade of hair. Brave hair. His own comb, like his compadarion, his bird. The Chicken Man has dusky arms. His Daddy always asking, Are you my son? You perhaps not from these loins. But I will keep you still. Gave him ice cream. Let him run. The Chicken Man's Daddy was a White Face. And is dead. The Chicken Man knew. Said Boo. Whispered in his ear. They came and took him. The Chicken Man watched from his hiding place. Was scared, was running, was just a knee-high and skinny like a stick, Daddy would fun him.

Now the Chicken Man bathes hisself in grasses. He is lying in the warm sun on the cool grasses. His chicken is with him. Daddy's chicken he found and took from behind a fence. In his asleeping Daddy came up like the burning sun, said yes, that is the one. A boy chicken, a Rooster, he keeps not saying right. The Chicken Man is a Rooster. Has hisself a comb, a yellow comb colored that way by Ghost, who used a bottle of the stuff to make it that way, like a blade of Sun, Ghost said. Chicken Man's chicken has a comb the color of blood. Feathers is black, shining. Chicken Man bathes in grasses of this field while his chicken pokes around. He won't go far. For the Chicken Man has a house for his chicken, if not for hisself, as always finds, yes, too, plenty of feed and water. He will feed his chicken first, he will make sure there is a little mountain of plenty. The house come apart like this, you pull off the top and there's a bowl, you fill with water, and you spread the feed in the grasses.

You don't make a show, the crowds will not like it. Dirty chicken they will say, dirty food in the clean bathing grasses. The Chicken Man has a box to keep things for hisself, what's in it changes. He has not looked in a while.

The warm sun is dropped down low, the day is cool, the grasses is just some warm, with little cool edges. Chicken Man lies there on his side, bathing in grasses. He will must walk all night to guard against them, the night hordes. But now he has made a place to lie down, and a yard around him for the chicken, strong black bird with shiny armor and a blood-red comb. Chicken Man's chicken will guard him.

Over across the street, other side of a fence, the crowds are eating ice cream. Chicken Man has had it, when he was knee-high, sure, but again not long ago. It was cool and sweet, too sweet, and it dripped and bathed him. He wore it that night and many days. He said here it is, you too, but Rooster did not touch it. Can't stab it with his hard-pecking mouth.

The Chicken Man wears a strange contraption, that thing for a horse, to make them pull? What did he do before? Before the blood-red comb and little mountain. He lifted, and put, lifted and put. His hard dusky arms. And Man like Daddy gave him paper and coins. Where they go? He feels them pockets lean. They lay flat as he bathes in grasses. Maybe he only saw it in his asleeping.

They watching us, the Chicken Man thinks. Crowds other side of the fence. Crowds this side with dogs. Lemme rest here and bathe, please. That girl, dusky arms too, she running around this circle that circles these grasses. It pleases him to see her, dusky arms like mine. But he knows the eye that watches him is not blind. That's a lie he told hisself. That no one was watching. They watching. They waiting. Chicken Man's chicken is a black dog. He got fight. We got fight. Let that girl be, dusky arms like mine. Let her run. Let her run that circle. She reminds us. We had a Mama too. Somewhere in our asleeping we will find her.

The Chicken Man is not my name, neither. I have a name I no can do out loud.

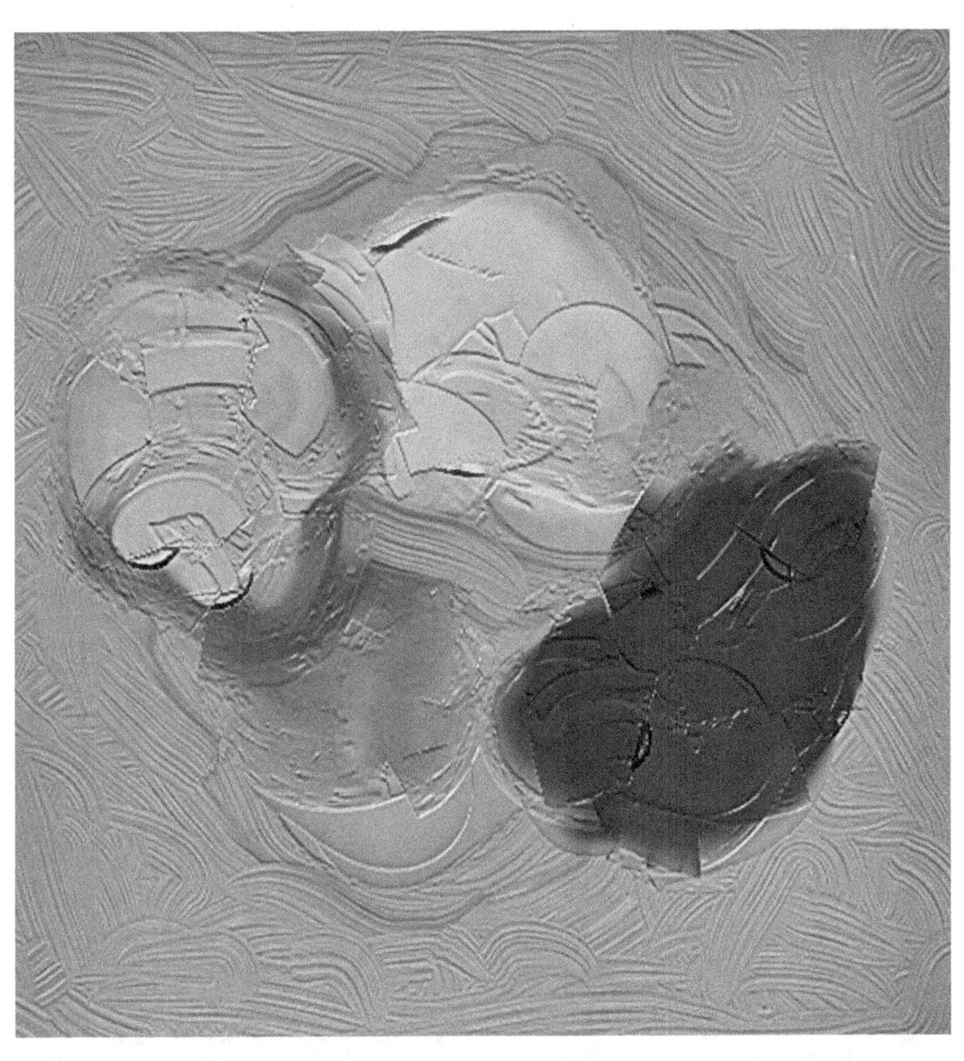

QUASAR BOTANICUS / IRWIN FREEMAN

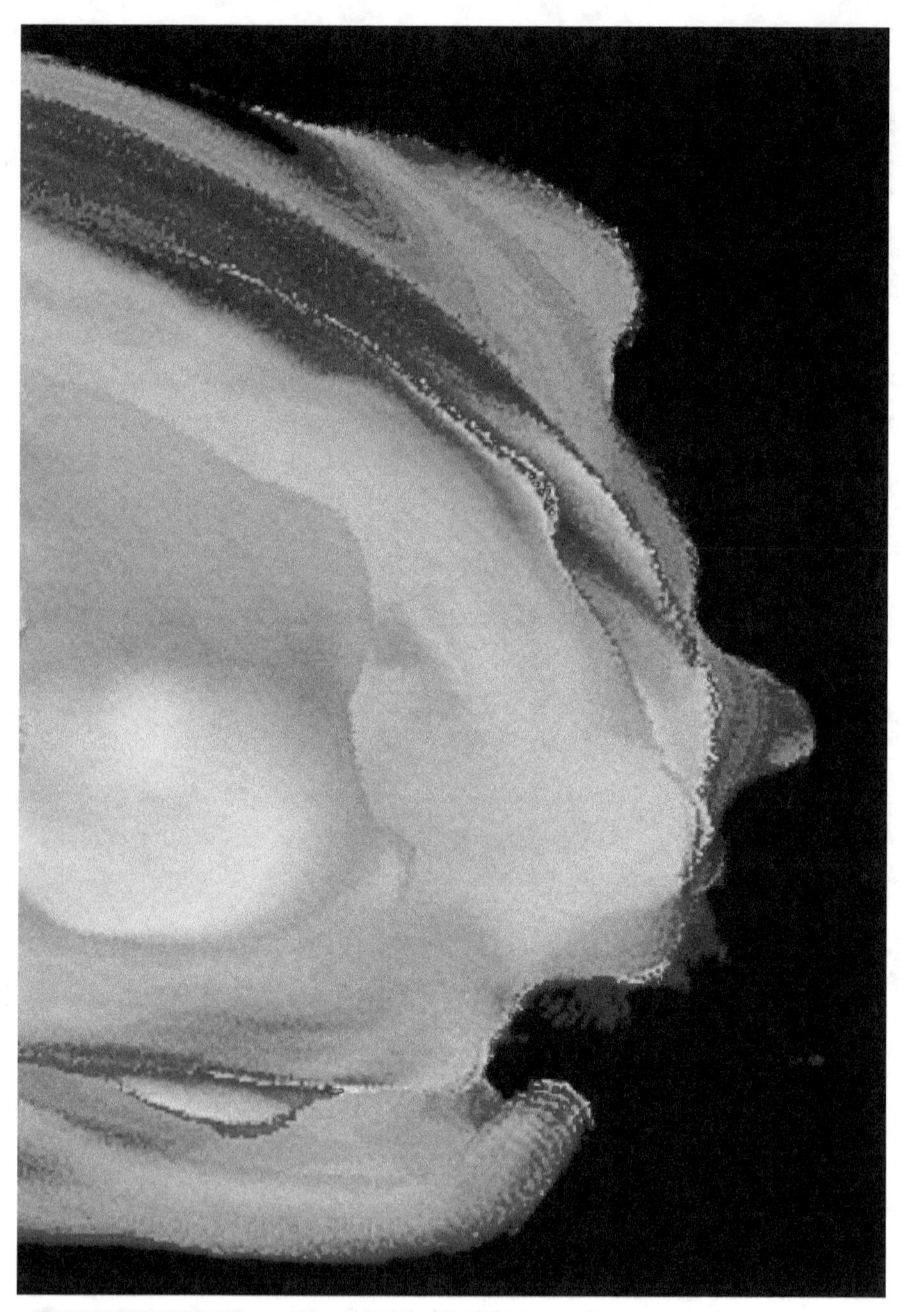

YOU, BLACK GOLD OF THE SUN

/ IRWIN FREEMAN

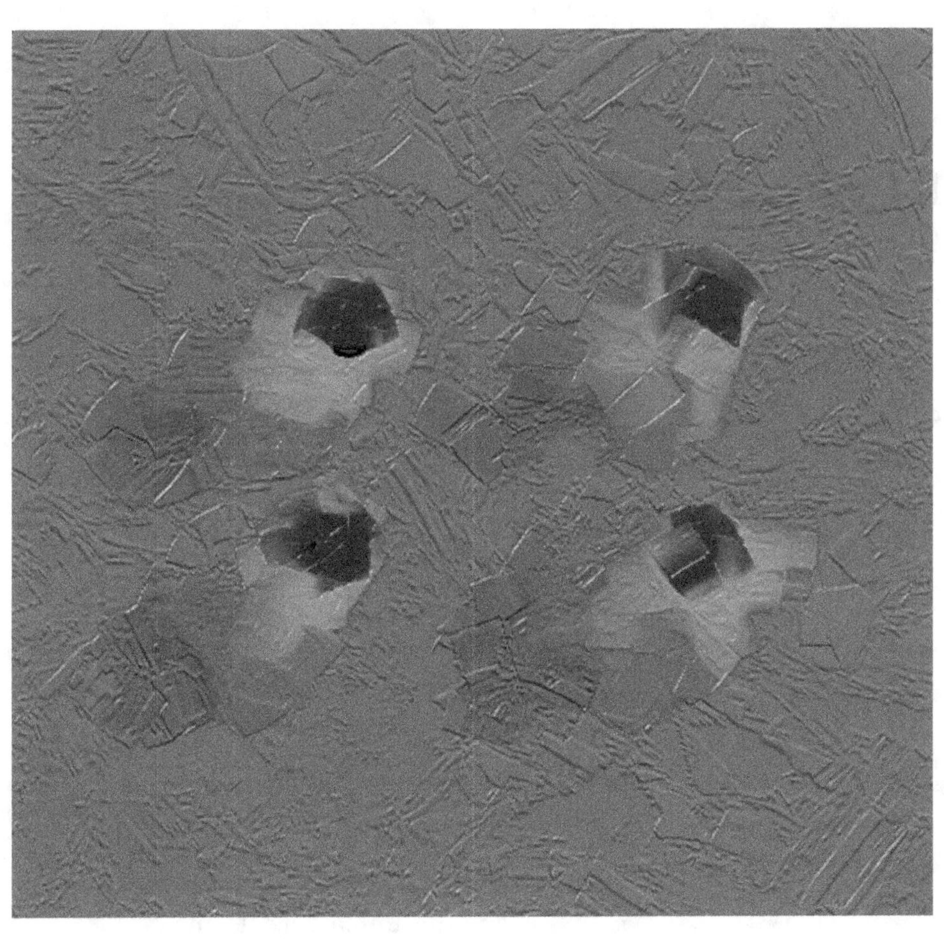

SOLAR WIND / IRWIN FREEMAN

Devotee of the Bog Witch

Leah Skay

Editor's Prize

I'm learning to listen and it is never quiet.

Mushrooms are growing antlers from the bones of frogs and the birds are screaming for sacrifice.

Trees along the marshlands lean towards the wind and flip their leaves; there's a storm coming, atom bombs and acid rain and the animals are fleeing.

I talk to the huddled herd and they tell me where to hide.

Let me wait under raised roots, wade to my knees in land too thick to breathe.

Cicadas speak the name of a dead god named Patience and crawl from the mud starving; I hold my breath and moss replaces my teeth. Hunger and waiting make nature's greatest behemoths.

I become home to dying things and ingest a thousand lives in one.

Let me fossilize and keep my skin; I crave
to die useful.

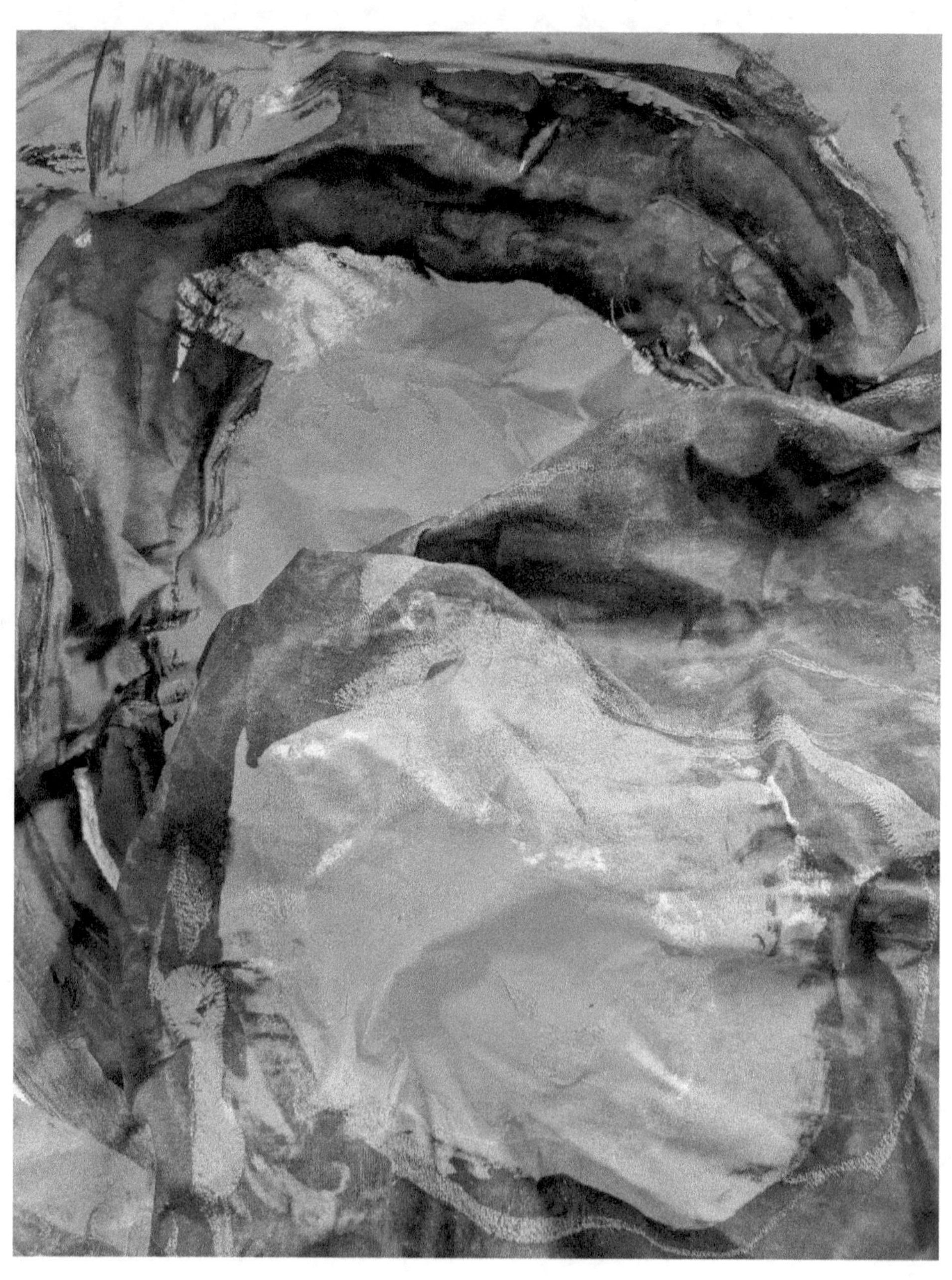

BINARY STARS / GARTH UPSHAW

No Diagnosis / Garth Upshaw

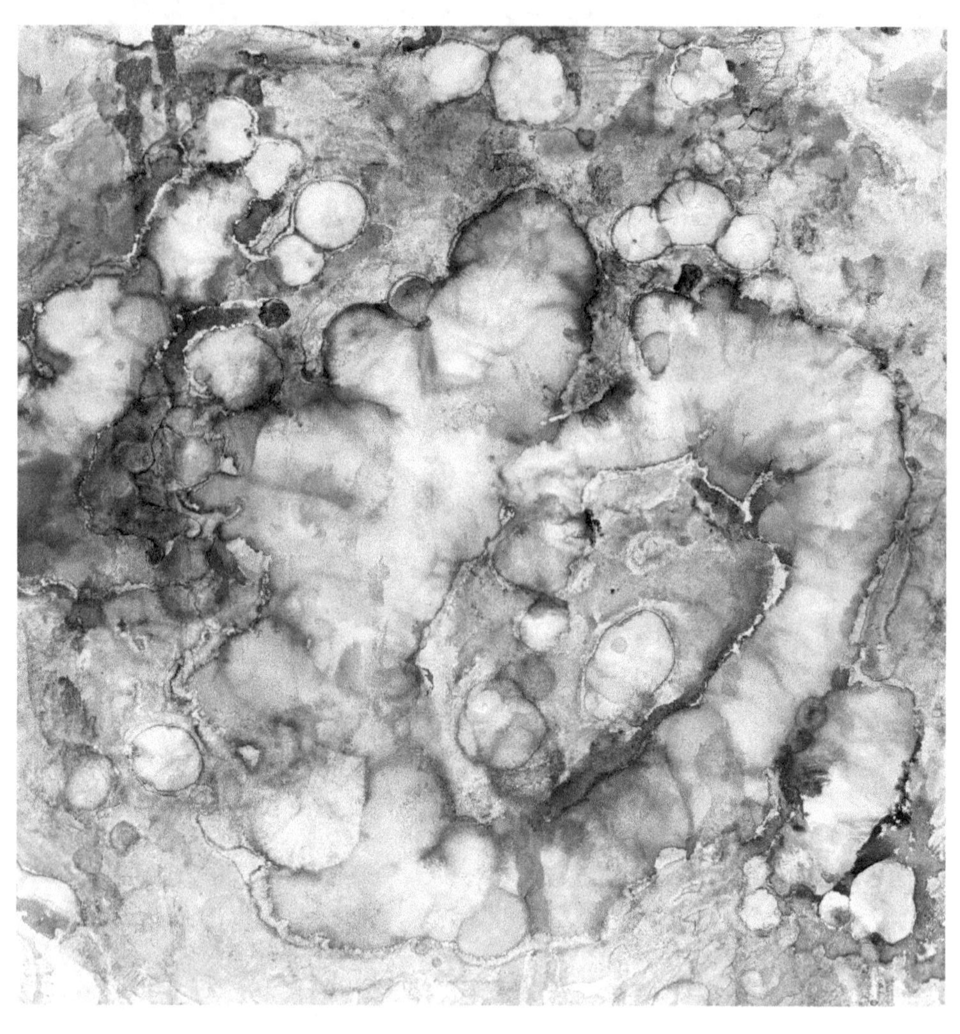

Color Penenda Ena 2024

/ Cynthia Yatchman

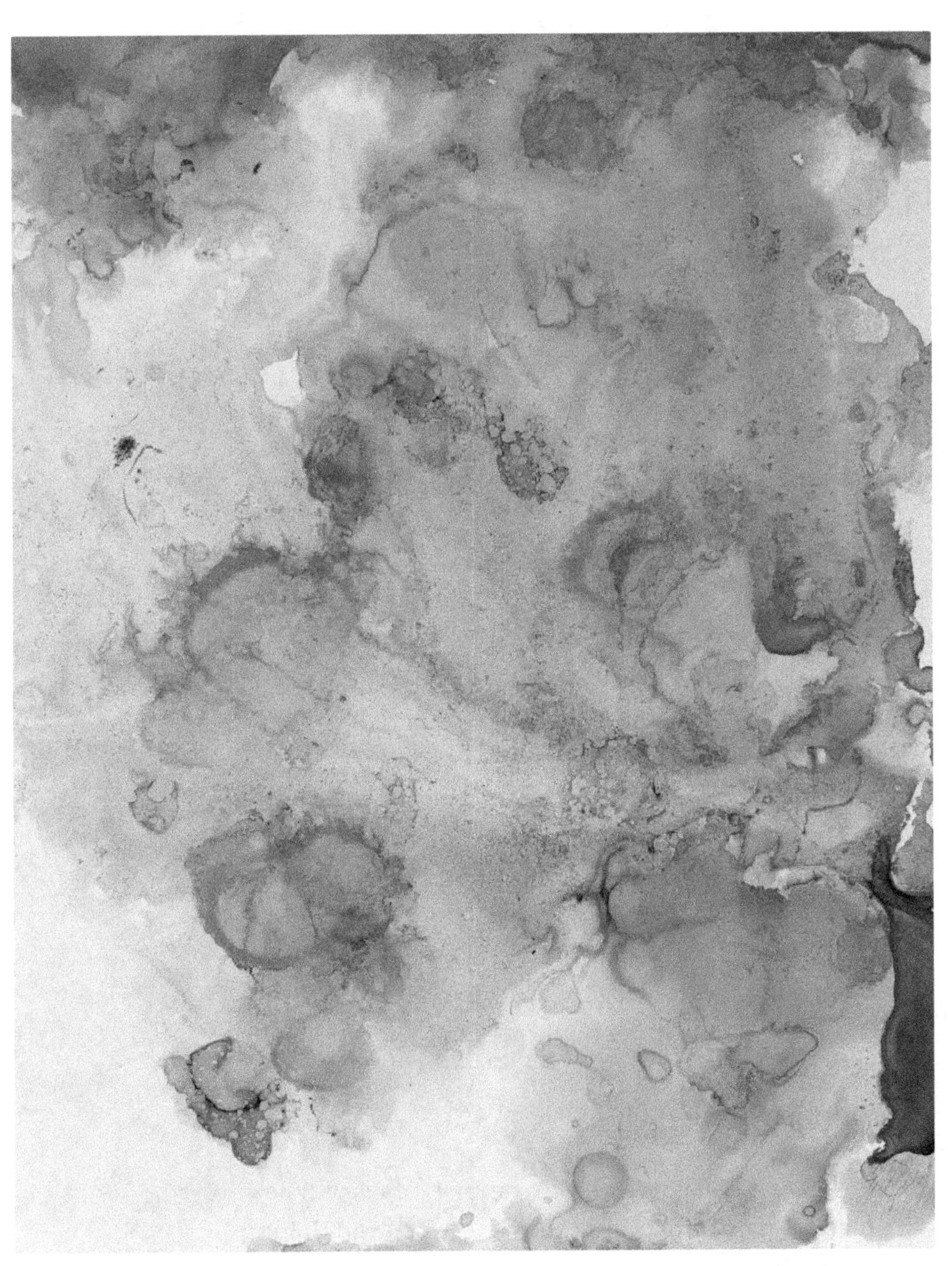

COLOR OKTO 2024 / CYNTHIA YATCHMAN

THE RED BARBERRIES ARE ALREADY RIPENING

RAINER MARIA RILKE

TRANSLATED FROM GERMAN BY WALLY SWIST

From *Book of Hours: The Book of Pilgrimage*

II, 32

The red barberries are already ripening,
aging asters breathe feebly in their bed.
Those who are not rich now that summer is gone,
will always wait and never own themselves.

Those who can't close their eyes now,
certain that a wealth of visions in it
only waits until the night begins,
to rise up in its darkness — :
passes on like an old man.

Nothing will come to him, no more days will be allotted,
and everything that occurs is a deception to him;
you, too, my God. And you are like a stone
that pulls him down every day.

Jetzt reifen schon die roten Berberitzen

Rainer Maria Rilke

II, 32

Jetzt reifen schon die roten Berberitzen,
alternde Astern atmen schwach im Beet.
Wer jetzt nicht reich ist, da der Sommer geht,
wird immer warten und sich nie besitzen.

Wer jetzt nicht seine Augen schliessen kann,
gewiss, dass eine Fuelle von Gesichten
in ihm nur wartet bis die Nacht begann,
um sich in seinem Dunkel aufzurichten: —
der ist vergangen wie ein alter Mann.

Dem kommt nichts mehr, dem stoesst kein Tag mehr zu,
und alles luegt ihn an, was ihm geschieht;
auch du, mein Gott. Und wie ein Stein bist du,
welcher ihn taeglich in die Tiefe zieht.

I LOVE THE DARK HOURS OF MY BEING

RAINER MARIA RILKE

TRANSLATED FROM GERMAN BY WALLY SWIST

From *Book of Hours: The Book of the Monastic Life*

I love the dark hours of my being,
in which my senses deepen;
in them, as in old letters,
I have found my daily life already lived,
and, like a legend, far and subdued.

From them comes knowledge that I have space
for a second timelessly broad life.
And sometimes I'm like the tree
that, ripe and rustling, over a grave
fulfills the dream that the boy who died
(around whom its warm roots crowd)
lost in sadness and song.

Ich liebe meines Wesens Dunkelstunden

Rainer Maria Rilke

From *Book of Hours: The Book of the Monastic Life*

Ich liebe meines Wesens Dunkelstunden,
in welchen meine Sinne sich vertiefen;
in ihnen hab ich, wie in alten Briefen,
mein täglich Leben schon gelebt gefundenund
wie Legende weit und überwunden.

Aus ihnen kommt mir Wissen, daß ich Raum
zu einem zweiten zeitlos breiten Leben habe.
Und manchmal bin ich wie der Baum,
der, reif und rauschend, über einem Grabe
den Traum erfüllt, den der vergangne Knabe
(um en sich seine warmen Wurzeln drängen)
verlor in Traurigkeiten und Gesängen.

I return home from my Silence

Rainer Maria Rilke

Translated from German by Wally Swist

From the *Book of Hours: The Book of the Monastic Life*

I return home from my silence,
within which I lost myself.
I was the singer, and God, the rhyme,
still resounding in my ears.

I will be quiet and simple,
and my voice stands;
my face lowers
to ardent prayer.
To the others I was like the wind,
as I called her trembling.
I was far away from where the angels are,
high, where the light melts into nothingness —
But deeply dark in God.

Ich komme aus meinen Schwigen heim

by Rainer Maria Rilke

From the *Book of Hours: The Book of the Monastic Life*

Ich komme aus meinen Schwigen heim,
mit denen ich mich verlor.
Ich war Gesang, und Gott, der Reim,
rauscht noch in meinem Ohr.

Ich werde weider still und schlicht,
und meine Stimme steht;
es senkte sich mein Angesicht
zu besserem Gebet.
Den andern war ich wie ein Wind,
da ich sie ruttelnd rief.
Weit war ich, wo die Engel sind,
hoch, wo das Licht in Nichts zerrinnt —
Gott aber dunkelt tief . . .

Love, Raymond / Emily Krill

It won't be quiet in the Houses, be it

Rainer Maria Rilke

Translated from German by Wally Swist

From the *Book of Hours: The Book of Pilgrimage*

It won't be quiet in the houses, be it
that one dies and they carry him on,
be it that on secret command someone
takes the pilgrim's stick and collar
to ask for the way abroad,
on which he knows you are waiting.

The streets will never be empty
of those who want to see you as that rose
which blooms once every thousand years.
Many dark people are almost nameless,
and when they reach you they are tired.

But I have seen the procession;
and have believed ever since that the winds blow
from the movement of their cloaks,
and are silent when they lie down — ;
so great is their walking in the plains.

Es wird nicht Ruhe in den Häusern, sei's

by Rainer Maria Rilke

From the *Book of Hours, The Book of Pilgrimage*

Es wird nicht Ruhe in den Häusern, sei's
daß einer stirbt und sie ihn weitertragen,
sei es daß wer auf heimliches Geheiß
den Pilgerstock nimmt und den Pilgerkragen,
um in der Fremde nach dem Weg zu fragen,
auf welchem er dich warten weiß.

Die Straßen werden derer niemals leer,
die zu dir wollen wie zu jener Rose,
die alle tausend Jahre einmal blüht.
Viel dunkles Volk und beinah Namenlose,
und wenn sie dich erreichen, sind sie müd.

Aber ich habe ihren Zug gesehn;
und glaube seither, daß die Winde wehn
aus ihren Mänteln, welche sich bewegen,
und stille sind wenn sie sich niederlegen — ;
so groß war in den Ebenen ihr Gehn.

From the Facing It Series

/ Jack Bordnick

Only Our Shadow's Know

/ Jack Bordnick

You from the Start

Rainer Maria Rilke

Translated from German by Wally Swist

You from the start,
lost love, you, who never arrived,
I don't know what sounds are precious to you.
No longer do I try, when the moment arises,
to recognize you. All the immense
images within me, landscape seen in the distance,
cities and towers and bridges and un-
suspected turn of events
and the mighty of those gods
who once traversed countries:
all rising to one meaning within me:
you, runaway.

Oh, you are the gardens,
oh, I saw them with such
desire. An open window
in the country house — and you almost stepped forward
towards me mystified. I found alleys, —
you had just walked them,
and the mirrors sometimes of the merchants' shops
were still dizzy with you and, frightened, mimicked
my abrupt reflection. — Who knows whether the same
bird didn't call through both of us
yesterday, separately, in the evening?

(Paris, winter 1913 - 14)

Du im Voraus

Rainer Maria Rilke

Du im Voraus
verlorne Geliebte, Nimmergekommene,
nicht weiß ich, welche Töne dir lieb sind.
Nicht mehr versuch ich, dich, wenn das Kommende wogt,
zu erkennen. Alle die großen
Bildern in mir, im Fernen erfahrene Landschaft,
Städte und Türme und Brücken und un-
vermutete Wendung der Wege
und das Gewaltige jener von Göttern
einst durchwachsenen Länder:
steigt zur Bedeutung in mir
deiner, Entgehende, an.

Ach, die Gärten bist du,
ach, ich sah sie mit solcher
Hoffnung. Ein offenes Fenster
im Landhaus—, und du tratest beinahe
mir nachdenklich heran. Gassen fand ich, —
du warst sie gerade gegangen,
und die spiegel manchmal der Läden der Händler
waren noch schwindlich von dir und gaben erschrocken
mein zu plötzliches Bild. — Wer weiß, ob derselbe
Vogel nicht hinklang durch uns
gestern, einzeln, im Abend?

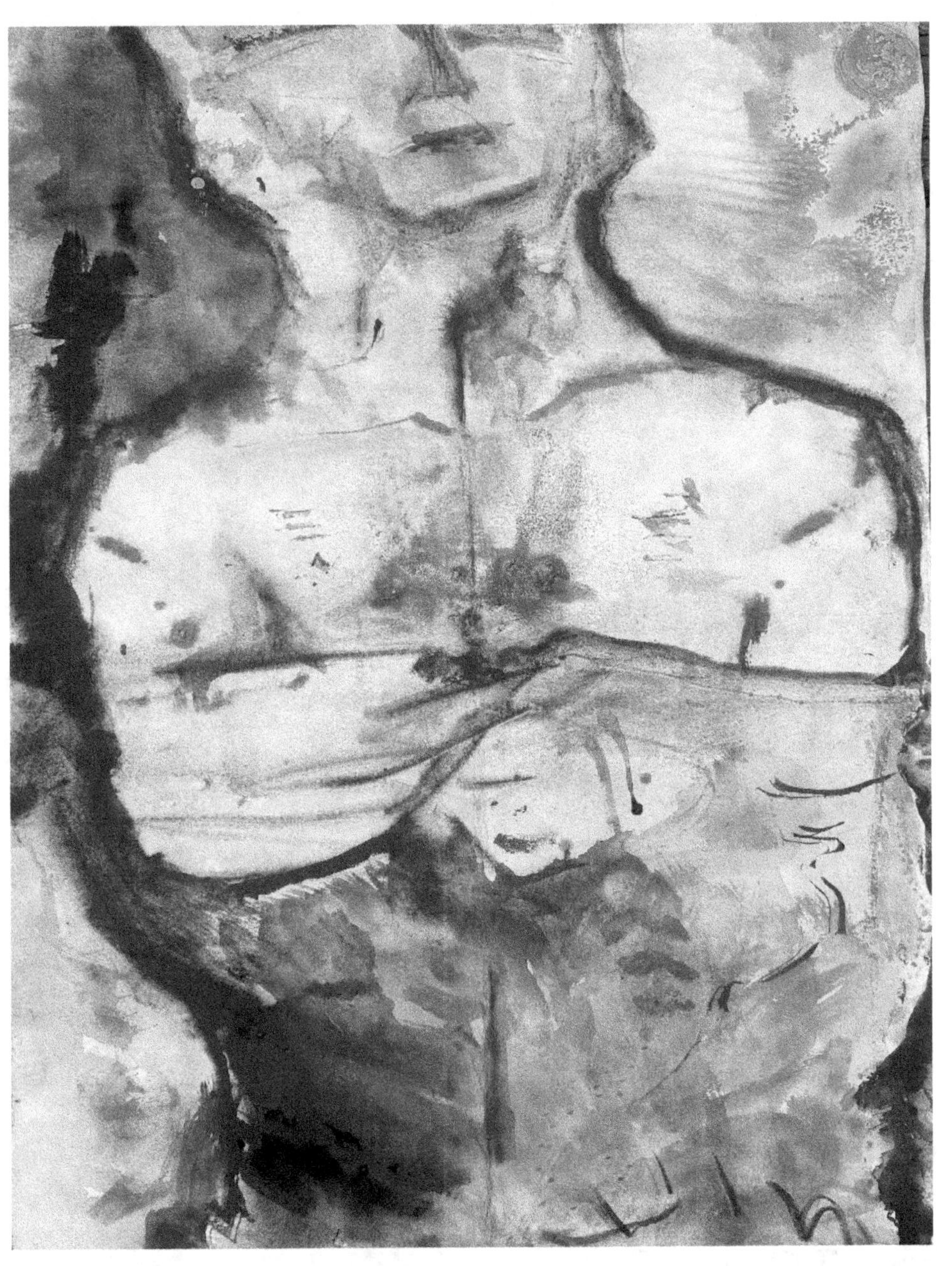

Blood and Sun and Steel Again

/ Dave Sims

LASTBORN SON — SUCKLING / DAVE SIMS

A Vile Body

Chad Gusler

and he was transfigured before them

The light come a cropper and bats swooped low over the stilly water, nipping day-drunk bugs from the dank air — one, two, and gone, over and again. The sun streaked long and then it were nothing, quick as a blink. But the man stood there in the burgeoning gloom, hands flat against his tight skirt, the slimy wood thick on his haunches. Trula knowed she could've worn his skirt better — her hips narrow as the Poor Fork linns that channeled white over the mossy stones — but she weren't fond how he leant against the piling, as if he thought himself a man of say. Hell, a man in a skirt weren't lofty to her.

He smelt like strawberry Jell-O and the sparse scruff on his chin like to gag her. But being the pastor, she said him anyways, offering her name. The sky was dark but faithful Orion held forth, Rigel's blue light blinking the black, and then he offered his own: Flannery. He was from afar, but his flat timbre said as much.

"Chicago?" she asked.

"More or less," Flannery said.

Trula patted her jacket till she found her cigarettes. He preferred candy cigarettes, but this evening's different, he told her, taking one of the two she forked out from a near-empty pack. She put a match to it, and after he inhaled, he folded down the piling till his knees framed his face and his junk flashed the stars.

"Shit," he said. "That's strong."

She averted her eyes and lit her own cigarette. His fledgling were snug down in its wiry nest between his pale legs. It shown lonesome, like it hadn't knowed a friend in ages, but she stuck out her hand anyways and Flannery grabbed ahold of it and lifted himself up. She'd yet to happen on a bonny cock, but she weren't exactly looking neither.

"You can spend a night," she said finally, poking his hollow chest, "and then you'll be off."

Flannery adjusted his wig, its burnished tips holding a crazy-ass flare. "A reasonable request." He held out his cigarette. "Want the rest?"

She did.

Hitch brung her morning coffee, and though his gait weren't right, not a slosh splashed over the cup's delicate rim. She'd bartered that cup off a dirty clod along the way to Black Mountain. It's raku, the boy told her, wiping his nose on the flappy arm of his gray sweatshirt. "And here's the Word of God," she said, tossing the extra she kept in the glove box for such occasions. "Thy silver is become dross."

The boy nearly dropped it, but that Bible weren't much anyways, the font between its shit covers stupid with curlicues. But how could she trash it given the nosy garbage man? The clod's daddy took it and sat in the tumbledown weeds, smoking a cigarette, eyes shifting across the thin pages. And from where she'd stood, it looked like he were raking through Jeremiah, maybe even pausing at one of that prophet's limp-wristed twines. Would it kill a prophet to be dick-sure for once? No, it wouldn't. And here she was now, fingering the pages of her morning Bible, asking Hitch if he'd looked after their patron, maybe give him a scoosh or two of coffee and a hot biscuit if you made any?

Hitch shifted his weight from his gammy leg and slapped flour from his apron. "He's an odd palmer."

"Queer as you," she said, closing her Bible, "but he suspires all the same."

He bowed till the oils in his curls were diamonds in the streaming light, and after he closed the parsonage door, she bundled to the window above the sink and peeked through the hanged spider plant: Hitch traiked himself across the boneyard, overselling his limp and leaving bent grass between the headstones that'd send Horse away with the fairies — Horse, her gardener, don't take no shit. Hitch slammed his shack door, and the wooden sign above it went crooked. Sequel, the sign showed, and she never twigged why it weren't fastened with two nails. He'd yoked his hut to Trula's church several years back, daubed its notched logs with mud and run a cord from the light pole in the parking lot to power his TV and toaster oven. The thatched roof sprung rye in the spring and mushrooms in the summer and leaks in the fall. He planted thyme at the entrance, which felt nice underfoot, though he gave her shit when she trod it barefoot.

"Looks like a cozy anchor hold," Flannery said.

Trula startled then settled. "A bulging tick on a bitch in heat." She let the spider vines fall. "He brung you coffee?"

Flannery raised his cup and took a sip. "Outside my door waiting," he said. "Good, too."

"I'll give him that," she said. "Don't know how he does it."

Flannery drew a chair and sat. "I'd say French press and a dark roast."

Mustard, her old tom, was clawing at the screen door and she let him in. "You get any sleep?"

"Very fine," he said, stroking the cat at his ankle. "What happened to his whiskers?"

"That idiot is drawn to fire," she said, "a moth to flame." Trula patted herself down before she realized Hitch hadn't yet brung her daily pack. Christ, smokes came later on biscuit days — when'd she learn? And would it kill Horse to brake at the TastyShak for a pack? She pays him good, but he'd kick up a fuss, swearing her body — a preacher's, no less — were the Lord's temple. As if his lungs weren't fucked from years underground.

She went to the sink and filled her mug, and when she turned, Flannery was dangling an immaculate smoke. "Jonesing?" he said.

"Where'd you get it?"

"Shirt pocket," he said, handing it across. "I keep a spare for desperate times."

Trula eased into her chair and flicked her lighter. "And last night weren't desperate?" she said, pushing Mustard away. The smoke cleared her smarts.

Flannery stood. "Desperation is a continuum."

She asked where was he off to, and he told her somewhere, but His portrait came first, because that's what he did every morning, without fail, a picture of Our Lord, thorns and all.

"You an artist?"

Flannery shrugged. "Some would say."

Trula's cigarette flared, then was soon drowning in the bartered cup. "I don't trust no pictures," she exhaled. "They're too still."

Flannery raised his penciled brows and slipped on a pair of cat eye glasses. They slid down his greasy nose, but he straight away pushed them up and drawed a tin from his purse. The rectangular box — about the size of a pack of Virginia Slims, her favorite when the giving were good — smelled like mints, and inside the tin were tiddly daubs of red, yellow, and blue: a trinity of colors where the candies once burrowed. A tiny block of paper nested on the inner surface of the lid. Flannery sketched a quick pic on the pad, Jesus knocking on an open door. She knowed that verse: Behold, I stand at the door and knock, the Revelator wrote. If any man hear my voice, and open the door, I will come in to him and sup with him. He that hath an ear, let him hear. Hadn't she opened that door eleventy times? She relinquished a penny in her good deeds jar, then an extra — bringing in the stranger deserves you two. And now the quart jug was nearly full, the year not even half-sewn.

Flannery was mixing his colors, his chicken fingers crackerjack with the brush, and Trula was tickled it were her door Jesus rapped on, the peeling panels showing the rotted wood and the line of ants up the frame. But why would Jesus bother knocking on an open door? He'd always seemed more barger than mannerly. Maybe Flannery knowed something she weren't privy to.

"What if a picture captures something the painter weren't expecting?" Trula asked.

Flannery tore the picture off the block and rested it in her hand. "Then the painting's real."

Jesus' thorns were glorified and the whole picture blazed. Flannery swiped some biscuits and opened the door. "This one will take some time to cure," he said before letting himself out.

Later, she told Horse that she weren't sure what to make of it.

Horse's rake clattered against the apple tree. He looked at the picture. "It's your door," he said, yanking on his mangled khakis. She turnt her gaze since she weren't keen anent the fibrous cicatrix that split his left nipple and bored into his pants and down his leg, a loose root looking for dirt . . . What a fucking scar! Still and all, Horse's good nipple stood erect in the sun, spoiling to fight its devil twin.

"But why's it open?" Trula said at last.

Horse's pants skid down till hip bones jutted like an exclamation. He weren't wearing his belt. Or underwear. She'd give him a belt and click three pennies to her jug. But underwear? That were his fucking business. And now she'd unclick a penny for swearing.

"You never been one to leave a shut door," he was saying, offering up a clove and yanking up his khakis.

The clove crackled and turnt her lips too fat for chit-chat.

On Fridays, Trula prepped her burial wrist with the Bible that lay fat on the altar next to the dead daisies. It were her precious King James, bound in leather, the one Pop had willed the morning of his passing. Its pages were brittle as onion skins, but its hulking cover contained the fearsome whomp of a casket lid. Over and again — *whumpwhumpwhump* — slamming the King James covers till Genesis cancelled Revelation. Till dusty eddies, startled in the rafters, swirled through Friday's final light. Till sweat clouded her sight. Ain't no body, holy or otherwise, able to creep from a Trula-shuttered box.

Hitch knowed to retreat on Fridays — the *whomps* were an aggravation — so he spent dusk near the Poor Fork's linns and pools, skipping stones and lifting rocks till the hellbenders fled. And when the bats came, Trula hollered his name then made his tea; and when his sweetness were restored, she sent him hutward, now off you go.

But she was soon beating on his door.

"I'm praying," he called out.

Trula jiggered his sign, but it went crooked anyways. "Open up." She banged again for good measure. There come a fissle inside, some cussing too, then Hitch stood at the opened door, hair a tangle of busted springs. She thrust Flannery's picture under his nose. "Look at this."

Hitch reached the light cord and squinted at the painting. "That palmer do it?"

"This door was open last night," she said, pointing, "and now it ain't."

Hitch turnt the picture over. "Initials F and O in showy scribble." He gave it back and made to shut his door, but she wedged it with her elbow. "What's it matter if it were opened or closed?" Hitch said at last.

She pressed her foot into his thyme. "Pictures don't move," she said, "and his crown is in pieces."

"Maybe this picture's slippery." Hitch swept her elbow and latched the door, then his voice come up muffled behind the wood: "Don't let it get your panties twisted."

But she worried her burial wrist at her kitchen table, kneading it with her thumb, her articulations not what they were. That picture weren't but a transgression tramping across gospel truth, she thought, watching her own image floating cold on the oily coffee in the bartered cup. She figured she'd be potty about a moving picture, but when it came down to it, there was something unsettling about a picture moving when you weren't looking, especially a Jesus one. She weren't one for surprises. She swirled the liquid till her likeness disappeared, then adjusted her hair and made note to have Horse give her a cut — he were shit-hot with his scissors. And now what was right in the world? Maybe stilly pictures were the better choice. She dumped her coffee in the sink, watched its aimless drain, then parted the hanging plantlets from her spider plant and rested the picture on the sill.

Just cause it were a gift didn't mean she had to gaze on it.

In the morning Shakey come clanking up the road on her purple bicycle. Trula had just settled by the window with her coffee and cigarette, and when she heard the racket, she pulled aside her grandmother's lace curtain. The chaffer's pots and spoons rattled from the green clothesline strung up inside the bicycle's chipped frame. Tin cups jostled in the wicker basket tied to the handlebars. Yellow tassels showed from the rubber grips — Christ, a pounce day, already the third this year. In the cart, amid the sponges and buckets and scuttles and rags, was a small bookshelf strapped to the cart with bungee rope. It were stocked with library castoffs, mostly stiff-spined books of poetry — fancy poets like Blake and Auden, Rich and Lorde — but a few magazines, too, mostly *Cosmopolitans* and *Vanity Fairs*, marcescent from wet thumbs and wetter gazes.

Shakey chimed her bell and leant her bike against the fence. She was soon kindling the hinges, easing Trula from her recliner— shit, just give me a minute, why the hurry? Trula opened the screen door, then moseyed down the stone pavers Horse had pulled from the Poor Fork. They were smooth and round — best for flattened arches! Horse told he — and still cool in the sleepy air.

"New powders!" Shakey said, hoisting herself onto the fence cap. She turnt her face toward the morning sun and rested there, tits perky as spring ramps. She wore pants sewn from ties traded by mine widows at the rag sale, and they clung to her hips like plastic wrap round a Sunday chicken casserole. Her water bottle were full of flowers, though it didn't keep her from sipping at the haze. When she finally hopped over the fence, she released the tambourine from her belt and banged it steady against her thigh. *Well there ain't no grave gonna hold my body down*, she sang. Trula brushed her toes against the plush moss running riot in the cracks between the pavers — it was nice to feel something pleasant, even it were only for a moment. Mustard nudged her ankle and throwed up a violent purr. *And when I hear that trumpet sound*, Shakey continued, *I'm gonna get off out that ground*. She suddenly chucked her tambourine, and the cedars limning the road hugged the racket in their berried branches. Trula's cedars were like that, loyal and given to necessity, not prone to heave her careless echoes across the folded mountains. No, Trula's cedars weren't fickle like the Poor Fork's nosy waters. And in the muffled silence, Shakey snapped up the fur flaps on her flannel trapper and sponged the pearly sweat from her hot cheeks. "So here's a mycelial pounce," she said at length, pulling a small beaker from her pocket and rotating it from her thumb to her pinky then back again. "Good for morning blues."

Trula ground her cigarette on a paver and flicked the ash with her toe. "Haven't had those for quite some time."

Shakey tossed the pounce over her shoulder; it sailed perfect over the pickets and landed in her cart. She pulled another vial from her pocket. "Okay, well here's a bit of bayberry powder," she said. "Good for fever dreams."

"Lost those long ago."

"Or as a douche for your bothersome discharge?" Shakey pulled the cork and offered up the vial. "Give it a whiff."

Trula took it and held it under her nose. "Smells like a candle," she said at last.

"Mix in a drop or two of Horse's firewater and you'll be good as new."

Trula shoved the beaker into her pocket, and it nestled there close to her lighter. "What else you got?"

"Just wait for this one," Shakey said, pulling a small box from her blue velvet shoulder bag and handing it across. "It's from a birder over Black Mountain, down in Delphie."

Trula pulled the blue ribbon and it flittered to the ground. She lifted the lid and there, snug down in shredded newspaper, was a taxidermed blackbird, its glossy feathers stiff as a wedding dick. She raised it from its nest, then nearly dropped the thing in horror; its body weren't just bird, but toy too: the birder had stuffed and stitched a wind-up dog into the bird's emptied chambers, a joining of flesh and plastic. It even showed the price on a bright orange sticker: a dollar ninety-nine from the Delphie dollar store. She shoved it quick-like into its nest and handed it over — that monster like to creep her.

Shakey clutched the box and laughed. "They're chimeras," she said, "and the birder's made lots of them — a robin transfigured with a china cat; a cardinal with a wind-up mouse; a titmouse with a rocking horse, though that one's a bit unwieldy in my juddery cart." Shakey pulled the blackbird from its shredded papers. She wound up its red mechanical legs then set it loose on the river-stone pavers. It stalled and Mustard like to hiss the monster back to hell before its four legs bungled it forward. But it weren't keen on provincing till its feet were purchased on the moss between the stones. Then it straight away fleeted but were on its back in a snap, legs kneading the warm air like tit-chuffed kittens making biscuits on their mama. When its vigor ran dry, Shakey scooped it up and nestled it to her breast. "Isn't it delightful?"

"If you like devilish things."

Shakey put it back in its nest. "So just the bayberry, then?"

Trula nodded and lit a cigarette, then tilted her chin to blow the smoke away. "Though I got a little something you might like," she added.

"You're looking to barter?"

"Just wait for this one," she told her.

Trula returned and handed over the picture of Jesus. It had moved, hidden there behind the loosely folded plantlets: now her door were shut and Jesus' crown more luminous than ever. But she went like the cedars and kept that secret close, even though her prickled skin might as well have blown her gaff. But Shakey was enamored, she could tell, because for once she went dumb. She pulled the painting from under the cedars' shadows and held it in the brightening sun. "There's a burning fire in it," Shakey said at last, "and it's exquisite."

"It's my door and savior," she said. "But the palmer who made it said it might take some time to cure."

Shakey fiddled the painting with her pinky. "Feels dry to me," she said, sliding the picture into her blue velvet bag. "And fair is fair, so I'm leaving you the robo-blackbird in kind." Trula tried her best to refuse, but Shakey held up her palm like a movie star and insisted she keep it, adding that she was throwing in the mycelial pounce for good measure, it will do you some good. Trula nodded, and after Shakey's clanking faded around the bend, she popped the lid and sent the ground mushrooms to the sky.

It came back on her a dry rain.

The bright day sky turnt to showers and the clouds, resolute as a bitch, sat low in the hollers, concealing cedar and oak and ash and maple. Trula donned the plush robe hanging from the hook behind her bathroom door and went to the porch swing. Fat water dripped from the swollen eaves, and Mustard jumped into her lap, jamming his zealous nose into her palm, but she were a mindless petter. The robe was pink and cozy and typically kept gloomy days at bay, but today she were sadder than the Man of Sorrows Himself. And that grief sopped her bones, like to cement her right there to the swing in fact, but Trula straightened her spine and anchored her toes; she were a preacher after all. But the chains scraped and groaned, and that was what hell sounded like, she decided.

Horse loped around the corner and up the porch steps. "You're liable to catch you a bug sitting here in the rain." He held his garden shears loose against his side.

She ran her eyes over the soaked lines of his body. He was wearing a shirt, but it were blurry against his wiry frame and the scar showed itself clear as day. His muddy khakis were hitched with twine. "My porch roof don't leak"— she tapped her head —"and now look who's dry."

Horse wiped his brows then pulled a plastic pint from his pocket. "That chaffer said you might need it." He put the firewater on the railing. "It's poured out from a bitch of a batch," he added, "so go slow or meet death."

Trula eyed the shears. "Nothing bigger?"

"My fingers got the palsies with things too big," Horse said, beginning to whinge.

His whine set her on edge — Christ, what was it about her that drawed all the dickless twits about? She ran her impatient fingers through her thick hair. "But they sharp though?"

Horse ran his thumb across the flinty blade, then nodded and snapped the shears shut, jolting Mustard from her lap. Horse asked why not use a normal scissors?

"Does it look like I got all day?" she said.

"But my tremblies," Horse was saying, and Trula wrenched the shears from his hand and snipped off a clump of her own hair. "See?" she said. "It's not hard."

And soon the steel felt good against her hot head. But how was it she could hear through skull bone, the blades that sheared buzzing in the core of her brain like a cicada? It was a grace and a miracle, she thought, this other way to hear, and then Horse cut her ear clean off.

Mustard dashed from the ficus and was on it in an instant. He bit into the fat lobe and ran off under the porch. Trula cursed and Horse ran after the cat — *here kitty-kitty-kitty* — then returned with her ear wrapped in his soaked shirt. "I didn't mean to split you," Horse said. "Here's your ear back."

Trula snatched the T-shirt and shook the loose ear into her lap, then clamped the material to her head to staunch the bleeding. Horse asked if it hurt, his voice a bare muffle. "There ain't much blood," he added, "so that must be good."

Trula grabbed the firewater and splashed a bit onto her wound. It burnt like holy hell, but she clenched her jaw and, tempering her spleen, knotted the shirt round her half-shorn head. When the pain lessened to a throb, she examined her ear, tracing her finger along its ridges and valleys. She'd never caught onto her ear being a question mark, how the valley arched a perfect S then swung back to her skull, washing up on her leather lobe. But she weren't surprised — wasn't that what a preacher's ear were for? Questions slide in and truth spews out.

"Best put it in the church freezer," Horse said. "Maybe they can stitch it back."

But that prospect were iffy; best make do with a simple hole in the head. She turnt her ear over, and it felt no more than a bark of cold fat girding a discount steak.

Shakey weren't a flashy sponger. Sure, she could fiddle at a goniometer and locomote like any other sponger, but she often fetched up at some hidden place — in the cedars upside the road, say, or behind the church where Horse liked to piss — and then finished her journey on a short foot; she hated making a scene. But tonight she come a sponging onto the porch swing: one second it were just a lonesome Trula and her cigarette, and a flash later, Shakey were there with Flannery cozy in her lap. Trula nearly shit herself.

"Took the fast ride back," Flannery said, adjusting his sock-filled bra.

Shakey shook her tambourine and blissed out to an old tune: *They whupped him up the hill*, she sang, *they whupped him up the hill for me*. Flannery joined in: *On the day when I was lost, they hung him on the cross, they whupped him up the hill for me*. After lots verses and some flat tripping, Flannery flopped into the swing and draped his arm around Trula. But he gave her a turn when he seen the bloody wrap and the crusty hair. Shakey chucked her tambourine into the wet grass, and the steady rainfall filled the rushing silence

"It's only a lost ear," Trula said at last, stubbing her smoke on the porch floor. "Not like I got the clap or anything."

Flannery plucked at the bloody rag. "Where'd it go?"

"To church," she said. "Horse put it in the deep freeze."

"And that's why God gives us two of everything," Shakey said. "It's a grace, really — two lungs, two kidneys, two ears, two eyes."

"Two by two," Flannery said, "but can you hear?"

Trula lit another cigarette. "About half as well."

"Some are born to sweet delight," Shakey said, "and some are born to endless night." She plunged her hand into her embroidered reticule and drawed out Flannery's picture. "Look what your old limn is up to."

The picture had moved again: now Christ were offering a loaf of bread at the closed door; now the ants were foregathered on Jesus' wrist, supplicating the round loaf. The crown of thorns shown terribly, so much so that the light cast an umbrageous figure against the door: there was a head and an ear, an arm and a torso, but she couldn't make out anything else.

"They are gone away backward," Shakey said. "Introibo ad altare Dei."

And Flannery translated: Go to the altar of God.

Trula weren't one for transubstantiation — communion were a symbol and nothing more; hell, she couldn't even say Eucharist — but she banged on Hitch's door and told him to put Christ in the oven. He pitched a fuss, claiming palmers are early to bed and early to rise, farmers who sow reap fragrant surprise.

"It's not even nine," she said, banging again.

"Make your own damn wafers," he called out.

Trula kicked his door and his sign went crooked. "You're as fucking useful as a mute in a choir."

Later, after much cussing and clattering from the church kitchen, whiffs of hot bread wafted across the boneyard and through Trula's window. Shakey was finally gone, having sponged herself back to Delphie, and Flannery, who was hoofing it to Tennessee after Trula's morning service, was snugged in the spare room. Trula were nursing a sermon, as she did every Saturday night, and the passage that come to her was from Paul's epistle to the Philippians: *For our conversation is in heaven, from whence we also look for the Saviour*, she read, *who shall change our vile body that it may be fashioned like unto his glorious body*. The chimera rattled its box and the sudden zizzing broke Trula from her brooding. She slammed her Bible against the table. The rattling knocked off. She lit a cigarette and thumbed the pages till Philippians showed itself. She read the passage once more, exhaled, and the robo-blackbird started up again. That monster were in a bad way, like it were pining for a walk, and Trula was all at once compunctious; she lifted the box from her shelf and pulled off the lid. The creature stared her up. She hadn't really noticed its black eyes. And even though it were dead, those eyes held her lively image — threw it right back at her, in fact, bandaged head and all.

What a way to refine resurrection.

Trula tucked the monster under her arm and strode to church. The sky drouk her head. Hitch's shack was so dark she let him be, fished her own key from her night-coat pocket and unlocked the sanctuary door. She traiked downstairs into the claggy darkness, and though the air was warm, her body always went stroppy til she flipped on the kitchen light — only then could she take a normal breath. Hitch's two loaves sat cooling atop the freezer next to Horse's contribution, a faithful quart of grape juice stomped from his gnarled vines set in the rocky slopes of Kingdom Come. She moved Christ and his blood aside, along with the blackbird, and opened the freezer. It gasped, and there, next to the spinach, waited her ear. Horse had wrapped it real nice, tucking in the plastic to keep the ear from burning. She picked it up then nearly dropped it seeing as it weren't a bit frozen; it had, in fact, softened the spinach. She laid her ear out and the radge lurched like a drunk, its gears droning like hornets.

"Hold your britches," she said, giving it a slap.

In the drawer next to the sink were Horse's Pez. She grabbed the abhorrent lamb dispenser with its missing eye — Horse's favorite — and stretched her ear around it till the lamb's mouth were jutting from her waxy earhole. It felt like eternity before it stuck, but the last bit of Super Glue from the wrinkled tube were good enough. She held it all in place with duct tape; it weren't pretty, but she decreed it art.

Trula found a bible — all the drawers had least one, all KJV — and turned to Isaiah 1. She unwrapped a bundle of Pez and began copying each word from that first chapter onto its very own Pez. She toiled late under a buzzing light, over seven hundred words in tiny script on over seven hundred Pez. When she were through, she shuffled the Pez and loaded twelve random words into the lamb. And what does the Lord require of thee? Then the lamb spoke, ejaculating candied words through her earhole. Trula knocked together a portent:

putrifying cucumbers
    delight not
    ass
give ear

scarlet sins
redeemed mouth
hear

Hungry now, Trula took a pinch of bread. But it were like raw chicken; the grape juice chaser iron from a split lip. She nearly kecked, but then she twigged God's shifty flow through the bread and juice, over stuff and substance, blurring the lines of all her shuttered boxes. He was the Three-and-One standing across the Poor Fork's linns.

Trula stood alone, but her God were queer.

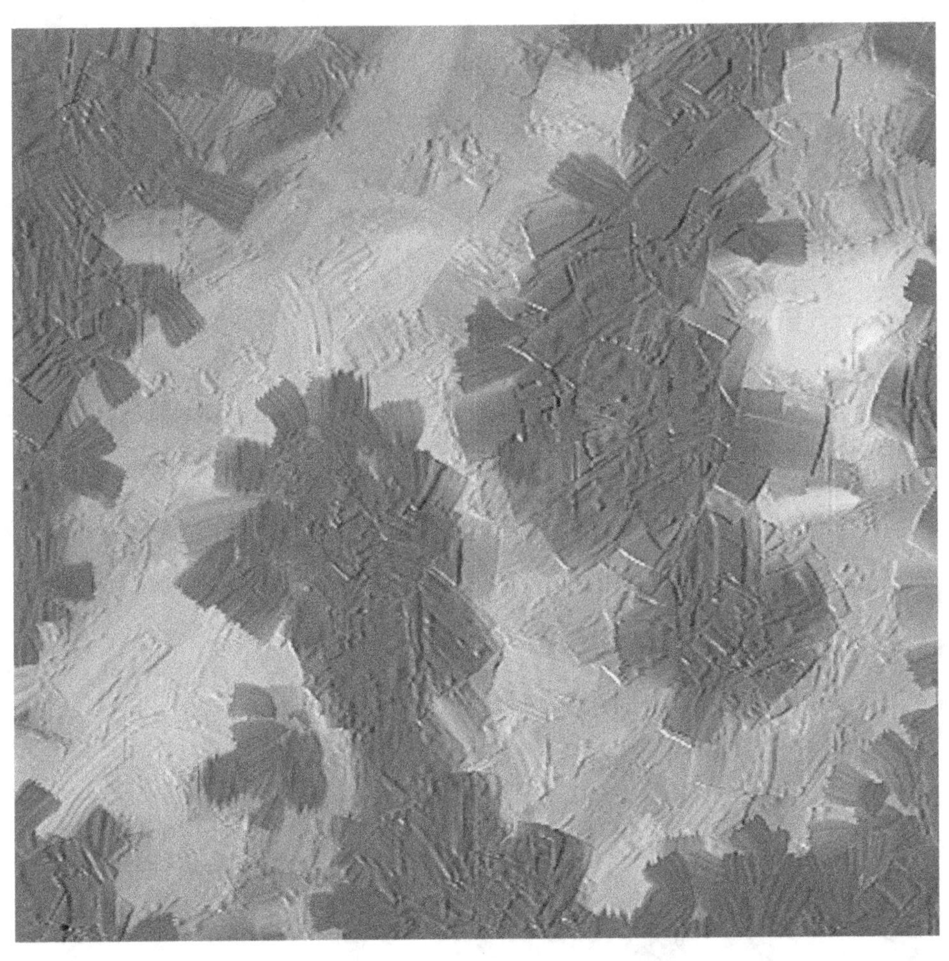

FLARE / IRWIN FREEMAN

TREMULA / ROBB KUNZ

Blueprint

Kristian Butterfield

Some nights there's something about the placement
of the lights beyond my bedroom window. They spell
out a message, some code I can't yet decipher,
but I'm working on a machine to watch the lights
and read the lines on the palm of the world.

It's not what this poem is about but I want to tell you,
when my grandfather died, I eulogized him in verse
and I regret it. I said something like:

> there is no sleep without
> a dream, no night
> without stars.

Good god. I was young but still –

Anyway, I'm working on a machine to suck the air
out of a room in case of a fire, and another to share
memories of dreams without vandalizing the feelings with words,

and another, to fight the overwhelming sadness of every ending,
two big fucking gloves that just *go* at the bedside, big and loud and simple,
trying their best to knock those feelings of inadequate usage back from wherever they came.

Connections / Elizabeth Yuan

RUMINATE / ELIZABETH YUAN

Subway Meditations

Aaron Carrot

Bleecker

Time was, I often sensed that something was about to happen. I was on the verge of something. I felt this when, for instance, I would ride into town on a Saturday night with my friends: a glowing dashboard, strawberry incense sticks, the Cure. The sense of my life unfolding; a sail hoisted to catch the wind. I have forgotten what came next; it was never exactly what I sought, but something always happened nonetheless. Now I seem to have undergone a subtle metamorphosis while looking the other way. I have unwittingly crossed a threshold. I can no longer recall the last time I sensed that something was about to happen. That feeling did not stop suddenly, like a road that leads to the edge of a cliff, but faded gradually, like the whistling of a train receding into the distance. In its former place I discover the feeling that something *has* happened. But what? That, also, I cannot recall. I was clearly not paying attention, as usual. But whatever it was, it left an irrefutable trace. There are crow's feet around my eyes.

Hunts Point

Sometimes I wonder if I have a parasite inside me. A writhing, blind, devouring worm that congests my sinuses, reddens my eyes, disrupts my bowels, and saps my energy. An horrific situation, no doubt about it, but one that still affords hope. Someday the masked avatars of science may find this worm and remove it, pulling it out of me like string cheese. Then I will be cured! There will once again be spring in my step, and my eyes will regain their blue. But what if this parasite cannot be removed? What if this worm is called *time*?

Whitlock

Let me tell you about that other me, the *romantic one*. He who stands entranced by clouds, yearns for women to fall in love with him, cries over imaginary losses, listens to Chopin on rainy nights, pours over antiquated maps, dreams of becoming a bird, takes pictures of abandoned buildings, and aspires to live according to artistic possibility. The *romantic one* is an incorrigible idiot, a sentimental fool whose stunted brain quivers in a vat of hormonal fluid. I would just ignore him if I could, but I cannot. For all his fatuous sighing, he is surprisingly strong and incredibly persistent. Take your eyes off of him, even for a moment, and he *will* take control. Despite my vigilance, it happens all the time. I blink and then *boom*, there he is, a braying jackass behind the wheel, driving us pell-mell toward annihilation. You have no idea how much damage he causes, and how hard it is to restore any dignity, whenever that fucking clown acts up. And what infuriates me beyond all measure is the fact that, while the *romantic one* is clearly my arch nemesis, he does not even know that I exist.

East 96th

I could go on about what might have happened during my so-called *lost years*, waxing melancholic on the inexorable demise of possibility. But there is always another truth. Things *did* happen during the lost years, and they were just as numinous as what did not. I wrote about Chaucer as a blizzard raged outside my little window. I drove my dying grandmother down a winding country road in Autumn. I watched my beautiful girlfriend bathe in a waterfall in a redwood forest. I walked under a glimmering emerald dawn in Seattle after having danced all night. The fact that these things were *episodic* and did not constitute any meaningful arc cannot be held against them. These things actually happened, while meaningful arcs are the greatest illusion of all.

Zerega

Self-consciousness is my archenemy. Ours is a lifelong duel. Always lurking in the shadows, his loreal pits locked onto the heat of my heart, he has ruined many otherwise happy moments with his venomous *awareness*. Sometimes I manage to evade him and experience the incandescent rush of life without reflection, but he soon finds me again, fangs dripping. Yet what would I be without him? Unrecognizable. His venom is inseparable from my blood. Vanity has its uses. It leads us to accept those parts of ourselves that we abhor but cannot banish. We cast out what we can; we grow to love what remains.

Middletown.

On a wintry Monday morning you ride your stationary bicycle and have a harrowing epiphany: *this is it*. Your destiny has come and gone. You watched for it all your life; yet you missed it completely because it did not rise in the east and set in the west. No, it came through some secret door, wove its inextricable web, and then stole away. Now you will never know your destiny's face, but you can plainly see what it left behind. Just look around you! *This is it!* It is not at all what you imagined, but then destiny and imagination never got along. To say they are archenemies is to vastly overestimate your imagination's might. While by far the more appealing of the two, your imagination doesn't stand a chance. Your destiny tramples it as a charging rhino tramples a mouse, without even noticing the squeal and crunch under hoof. But do not fear; your precious little imagination will survive. Its resilience is legendary. Even now, with a shattered spine and bloody mouth, it still sings its sweet, impossible song.

BIG APPLE MONTENEGRO / REX WILDER

AI ASSISTED

From the Transitory Space Series

/ Leah Oates

HOUSE OF CANNIBALS

ANITA CABRERA

This is the house in Messajanes where they assigned me the bedroom with no window or door that closed. This is the house where the Australian painter a breath older than thirty whose works are auctioned before brush touches canvas offered to switch rooms and gave me the one with a window and a door that closed. This is the house where the painter and I were instructed not to feed the feral cats that invaded the patio because the German actress and playwright who lasted only three days kept laying out saucers of milk and food scraps and now we had fleas and cat vomit and turds. This is the house where I felt all sixty-two years of myself on the second day when the rock-and-roll legend called to invite the painter to the concert in Lisbon with backstage VIP passes and the painter asked the five other resident artists in town, all under thirty, but not me, to join him. This is the room with a twin bed across from the street-level window. This is the window that the neighbor with the silent Brazilian wife blocked each night with a different car. This is the wall next to the window where I taped a piece of drawing paper. This is the paper on which I scribbled tasks and deadlines, and schedules of yoga, biking and dance so I wouldn't go crazy alone in the room all day writing what hurt. This is the house where the artist quoted the rockstar who said you've got to "cannibalize your pain." This is the desk where I sat and finally wrote about the night I started to kill my mother and did not let myself walk away until it was all out in one form or another, until my muscles twitched against the wooden chair at the flimsy desk and a first draft was born. This is the house where each day I passed the painter in the studio off the kitchen working seven hours straight making canvases and colors and drawing bases and painting for shadow and form and jerry-rigging a makeshift crutch to lean his arm against. This is the house where I sprang up from the chair to go out with the cats on the patio and sit on a splintered wooden stool and stare at the blue and white *Nossa Senhora do Remedios* cathedral up on the hill and bummed cigarettes from the painter and listened to how he learned more about light and depth from a copy of *How to Paint Like the Old Masters* he found at a garage sale than from all his university art classes. This is the house with the patio where I crept each morning with a threadbare hand towel as a yoga mat and killed fleas and swatted flies and practiced breathing. This is where I did a forty-minute vinyasa yoga stretch with Adrian on YouTube on the warped slats of deck or practiced dated choreography memorized from years of dance classes. This is the house where the Brazilian wife of the unsmiling man with many cars peered over the wall while hanging laundry when I was dance stretching to Patti LaBelle's *When You Talk About Love*. This is the house where the young painter and I listened for truck horns, ran out to the street, and waved down vendors selling vegetables and fruit, bread and cheese. This is the house where the painter prepared dinner for us both each night because, according to his fiancé on speaker phone calling from Sydney, he really loved cooking for other people and I shouldn't feel bad about eating it. This is the house where I sat outside with the cats in the dark listening to the young painter who, as the evening wore on and the beer ran out, repeated over and over how he couldn't believe how "you" Americans were allowing mass shootings and the reversal of Roe vs. Wade. This is the house where each morning I woke to twenty emails asking for money to help stop mass shootings and the reversal of Roe vs. Wade. This is the room where I hit buttons to sign petitions and send $5 or $10 because I was too far away to make campaign calls or write postcards. This is the house where I submitted rough writing and counted scores of rejections and one acceptance for a piece I didn't love. This is the house where I parked the borrowed bike with loose brakes. This is the bike I rode at dusk down to the square then up to the top of the hill to sit in the shadow of the church and take in the village below me. This is the house where the young painter and I invited the artists from Belgium, France, Bulgaria and Utah to share dinner out on the patio. This is the kitchen where I tore wilted leaves of romaine and listened to the welder describe meeting her new beau on Tinder and sang with the photographer slicing tomatoes. This is the house where guests brought wine and homemade savory tarts and fruit tarts and vegan sushi without seaweed, where, perched on tiny stools and broken chairs beneath the clothesline, we drank tea after dinner and cracked open pistachio nuts dispensed in cans for one euro from a machine in the bar with the pool table. This is the town where people referred to me as *La Espanola* and I was not going to correct them. The town where the painter ran up to the corner cafeteria for cigarettes after dinner and bought a round of beers for everyone and then consumed the multitude of beers paid back to him. This is the house where the artist wobbled home over cobblestones and recounted how the townspeople had thereby christened him *El Presidente*. This is the house where El Presidente showed me the Instagram clip of him proposing to his girlfriend who models for Vogue and described the engagement ring he designed that contained his little sister's ashes. This is the house where one night I smoked too many of the cigarettes I had bought for the artist while out on a bike ride and almost fainted the next morning after practicing choreography on the patio. This is the house where the artist knocked on my door and asked if I was okay and left me a plate of cut up fruit and toast and eggs covered with a napkin on the kitchen table. This is the house where I and the painter half my age who wore the trousers to a Gucci suit designed just for him with no shirt but a full apron watched a UFC tournament from across the world on a phone screen because he and one of my sons back in the States both trained. This is the house where before I left, the artist and I sat out on the patio later than usual, he this time cold sober. Where he wondered aloud if his drinking so much might have something to do with his sister's death. This is the house where I paused. Where I did not ask the question, but instead waited, the answer already wafting up in spirals strangling the stars. This is the house where I stayed anonymous because I did not want to seem to proselytize sobriety. This is the house where I thought about telling the young artist that I had finally written about trying to kill my mother. This is the house where we cannibalized pain and didn't speak of it. This is the house I left after hugs and kisses when the painter and the other young people gathered around to see me off. This the house I left far behind before I ever saw the YouTube video of the painter accepting an award and asking the audience to indulge him as he used the moment to give voice to his sister, his best friend, whom he lost to suicide. His sister, he said, who would have told us all to support one another by listening and asking hard questions. This is the house where I danced in the morning and sat with the cats and smoked with the painter and ate with young artists. This is what came out of the room with a door and window and piece of paper on the wall telling me to sit and listen. And write down what happened.

To Exit the Modern Labyrinth

/ JC Chen Henderson

On the Wings of a Gyrafalcon

/ Robin Young

Dean Martin

Jennifer Seigle

Goldilocks Zone 2023 Finalist

Sitting in a wine bar at JFK in late November I am watching the planes execute elaborate choreography on a large scale: wings passing wings, hulking centers meeting jetways, doors opening and closing, passengers bound for . . . . The world. *Spatial relationships, movement, architecture*: it's all happening in real time.

Behind me a woman in a shiny pair of expensive boots has absentmindedly ordered a glass of "red." But she's not here for the wine. She is searching for something else. A plug. She is searching for a plug.

I wonder — does she see the fleet of police cars surrounding this flight? Does she see the swirling and rushing? Without my glasses they create an urgent kaleidoscope of red and blue. Colors flashing in the night like the holiday lights that will soon surround us. On the runway a jet is rolling again. Slowly. *Tempo.* It bounces a bit on the uneven pavement. *Movement.*

I am tempted to get my glasses. To find out what the lights are all about. There. Focus. Clarity. The kaleidoscope is gone. The lights are clear. I still don't know what's happening. Do I need to know? Do I want to?

Something about those black and whites, lights and sirens blaring, in the heart of New York, will always give me this feeling. Terror — muted, but present. Is that the defining emotion of my generation? A dull sense of dread in the pit of my stomach. Is this the next one?

Back at the wine bar Dean Martin is telling me to pick myself up and dust myself off. I have already picked myself up so many times. More times than I can count now. And the dust never comes off. Does it? I wonder, am I starting over now? Am I just taking a break? Am I just roaming the country drinking overpriced wine in airport bars? I am deeply ambivalent about this.

Deeply. What is it that I'm afraid I'm supposed to be? What if I am not supposed to be anything? What if I am just here — until I'm not.

I continue drinking and the lights keep swirling outside and the world appears to be ending on the tarmac. Dean is crooning about landing on the right side of life. "Just forget that you're a worrybird . . . ." Easy for you to say, Dean.

Red blue red blue against the night sky. JFK is surprisingly quiet for rush hour on a Friday night. It's November. Doesn't anybody go anywhere anymore? Don't I?

Remember when flying felt glamorous — and vaguely fancy. I remember feeling a tremendous sense of power the first few times I pulled my roller bag through the terminals at Logan and LAX. Look at me. Little me. Making my way through the world. I'M HERE! I'm gonna be somebody.

But maybe I'm not. Because it's twenty years later and I'm still just little me. Making my way. Pulling my roller bag through the world.

The woman behind me in the fancy boots has been nursing her glass of "red" since the dawn of time. After crawling on the floor under the table she has managed to plug her phone into a light pole. I admit that I'm impressed with the determination. Now that she has reconnected to the world she is telling someone that she "feels really bad about it." I don't think she does. I don't think she feels much of anything. I wonder how many more generations of humans will actually feel things.

The lights are still there. More black and whites now. A big ladder truck.

I am jealous sometimes, of the people who don't feel so much. I wonder what it would be like to walk through the world without the fear that I have missed the moment, missed my calling, missed . . . . I don't even know what. What was I supposed to be chasing? I didn't get a map so I chased it all. And then started back at the beginning. Everything changes. And yet I always end up with the same terrible bob haircut. How is that possible? Life is a cabaret. This haircut is not.

The parade of police cars are leaving. Screaming away with lights flashing. The ladder truck is slowly packing up behind them. What happened? I wonder. Did you make it better out there? Did I? But it doesn't matter. Listen to Dean. Pick yourself up. Board your flight. Keep pulling that roller bag. Because you're not ready to put it down.

In the Woods Once Upon a Time

/ Robin Young

Goldilocks Zone 2023 Best of Art

Revenant

J Carraher

Goldilocks Zone 2023 Best of Poetry

the time grandmother
appeared as revenant, a
shadow cast under the pale
arbor encrusted with dead
vines falling across
stiff snow, she asked if
i had seen her lost
body. i replied
that I hadn't, but
remarked that sometimes
her soul blew this way
and that from the old, sagging
clothesline where she used to hang
our wet swimsuits, mid-summer.

Mis-en-scéne

Kathy Flann

Goldilocks Zone 2023 Winner

Mise-en-scéne:
How I Turned My 100% Perfect Rom-Com Moment
into a Total Horror Movie

For a year, I'd felt butterflies with Graham, the kind of sparkling, gossamer attraction everyone says they want. But when he finally reciprocated my interest, I discovered the problem with butterflies — grand gestures startled them. They might flutter anywhere.

I'd just returned from my night class, *Holiday French*, when the iron doorknocker split the silence in half, jolting me out of my textbook. Maybe the bang seemed ominous simply because I'd devoured so many romances and dramas set in places like Golgotha Village, where I now lived — a single row of ten skinny houses built in the 1600's, perched above a small city and the Irish Sea. "Laundresses" had once lived in these homes because the wind on the hill had been ideal for drying clothes. The gusts would also have swayed the bodies of condemned inmates, who were marched up here from the castle for execution at the gallows. Nowadays, though, life here was quiet, and I studied the door before I got up and opened it.

Graham stood there in the dark. At the threshold, he stood close to me, the way he always did, closer than people usually stood. I gaped, blinked up at him. He wore a navy shirt with his fire brigade company logo and navy pants — suggesting he'd come straight from his shift.

He lived three hours north, on the coast beyond Glasgow. We'd had an extended almost-a-thing, and he was almost interested. I'd always been the one to visit him, and his ambivalence held my attention like a gem rotating in a case.

Neither of us spoke. His eyes, ice blue, held mine, and even in the dark, he had that hint of rose at the cheeks. With the black hair, he looked too damned Scottish to be real. Then — as if he were not a figment of my imagination — he hunched his shoulders to protect against the chill, and he smiled his cheeky smile.

Something finally clicked. "Oh," I said. "Come in." And I moved aside.

I shut the door, gestured to a seat, and offered him water. I steadied my nerves in the kitchen while I ran the tap, staring at the wall and taking yoga breaths, trying to temper my giddiness. He'd probably just swerved off the A6 on his way to visit someone, I reasoned, or to pick up his little nephew from a school trip.

The last time we'd seen each other had been some weeks earlier — we'd met up at a bar the evening before my flight to France, where I traveled periodically to visit friends. Glasgow was my nearest major airport. He'd arranged for us to stay at the home of an acquaintance who was out of town. That night, as always, I donned a full set of pajamas, as if they were a Hazmat suit. In stories, heroines often allowed themselves moments of wild abandon, which seemed fantastic in theory. But sometimes casual hook-ups made guys like me more, and then a dread would flood my body with an urge to flee. Or if physical intimacy didn't make that didn't happen, and a guy was indifferent, I'd be the one hurt. It seemed a no-win situation — if they liked me or they didn't. I told myself that casual wasn't for me — I needed a stable situation with the right person. Still, he and I did make out *a lot*, even if it was rated PG.

I brought the glass of water to where he waited. He perched on a wing-back chair, hands clasped on his knees, as if he didn't know what to do with them.

"Cheers," he said, British for *thank you*, and he drank most of it down. Then, he looked around the tight room and the fake logs glowing in a fireplace designed for coal. He'd never been to my house. The previous summer, he did drive me to the job interview that got me here. He'd liked the city. "I could live here," he'd said. Then he made a jokey *yuck* face. "As far as *England* goes."

I sat down, returning to *French for Dummies* — I'd been searching for phrases to transcribe in my notebook. I yearned to converse for real in France, but so far could only order a sandwich and count to 100. The book had examples like, *Avez-vous un seau en plastique?* Do you have a plastic bucket? *Quelqu'un m'a vole mes poireaux.* Someone has stolen my leeks. *J'ai tout perdu!* I have lost everything! I'd been contemplating that last one right before the knock. Maybe I could repurpose it to explain that I'd moved a lot, living now in my 25th home. The connotation wasn't quite right, but at least I'd be venturing away from leeks. I circled it now.

I said nonchalantly, "What are you doing here?" Maybe he'd let slip some new clue about his feelings.

Graham put the glass on the end table. He leaned forward on his elbows and hung his head, the way a sick person might lean over a boat railing.

I thought, *Is he okay? . . . .* And then, *Oh God, he's here to dump me?*

He popped up and smacked his hands on his legs. He looked me in the eyes.

"The thing is, Kathy — I love you."

"What?"

"I love you, Kathy. And I want you to be my girl."

"You *do*?"

I blinked from the settee. He'd driven here . . . actually for me? I wasn't sure which stunned me more — his change of heart or his totally sincere and sweet use of *my girl*, like we really were in a movie.

"I thought we were in a 'gray area,'" I said.

We had discussed this in the bar the last time. Or rather, *I* had discussed it — after a second drink. I said I wanted to start dating in earnest. He eyed the floor like he might crawl under his stool. I hadn't wanted to hear him say that he didn't think of me *that way*. Again.

To preempt it, I'd said, "Let's just say we're in a gray area and leave it at that."

He had nodded over his whisky, and that had been the end of the discussion.

"A *gray area*," he said now with a snort. He rolled his r's and he pronounced it like greey ear-iy-ah. "There's no such thing as a gray area. That's total shite."

I'd been baffled for so long — he'd taken time off work to be with me during each of my job-hunting trips to the UK. He'd brought me home to his family several times. On one trip, he produced from his suitcase a book of Robert Burns poetry he'd brought for the sole purpose of reading it aloud to me — which he did as we lounged on a four-poster bed at a B and B in Edinburgh. To say I pined for him would have been an understatement, like saying that "Four Weddings and a Funeral" was *a little bit* devastating or that peak Hugh grant was *slightly* charming.

The next plot point in our story, I knew, was for me to burst into tears, throw my arms around his neck, and say *I love you, too*. Cue the music. It was simple.

But somehow, I couldn't. My heart raced, beating faster and faster, and not in the fun way. It seemed to expand to supernatural size — more like something from an M. Night Shyamalan story than a romance. What was happening?

He waited, studying the red carpet. "Yeah . . . so . . . ."

I banged on my own glass. *Speak, you fool! Say anything!* Suddenly, Graham seemed the protagonist here, a heartbreakingly vulnerable John Cusack holding up the boom box in the dark to Ione Skye.

"Well," he added. "There you have it."

I felt my lips go white. But then finally, muscle memory kicked in, and words began to form. And what came out was worse than any nightmare.

I said, "How are your folks?" and the, "Work good?"

Dear God. *Small talk?* No, no, no, no, no.

The roaring electrical noise of my heart drowned out every awkward thing that followed.

That night, we lay next to each other on an air mattress — my real bed was a twin. We kissed a little and then turned away from one another. He soon snored softly. I rolled over and studied his shaven head, the black stubble. Nothing had changed about my attraction. This trans-Atlantic situationship ticked so many squares on my rom-com bingo card. Wasn't this next step what I wanted?

I understood that I'd balked, of course — what I wouldn't suspect for a long time was that maybe it happened because I'd had so many surprises in my life already.

My own parents' whirlwind romance culminated with a quickie ceremony in Vegas. The only constant was change — divorce, new partners, twelve homes before the end of high school. My brother died in a car accident. My teen-aged aunt shot herself in the head, survived, and came to stay with us as she adapted to her paralysis. But these experiences were not surprising anymore, just scenery that passed when I fluttered around my mind. If I'd alighted anywhere, I might have seen how these formative years shaped my inner landscape. Real connections seemed always doomed to metamorphize into painful loss.

The problem with "the one" was that there was only one. It was a risky number.

I didn't have phrases like *avoidant attachment style* or *escape response*, just a feeling that I could have Graham *or* safety. Not both.

In the morning, we walked. For a British winter day, the clouds were high, and when the sun rose at 8am, a weak blue sky materialized. Normally, we bantered, even if it was just to quote lines from *The Simpsons* back and forth. He'd have that wry smile, that glint in his eye. Today, though, we walked in silence. The journey to town was three quarters of a mile downhill, and the views stretched to the coast. The sky was pink behind the castle turrets.

He marveled at my choice of words. *Pretty*, I'd said. He had repeated it. "Pretty." And he wasn't teasing me this time. He smiled in a genuine way, that adorable gap between his front teeth. "We wouldn't use that word to describe a sky," he said, wistful, like he wished he could describe the sky that way, at least unselfconsciously.

"What would you use it for?" I asked.

He gestured to me. "A person. A pretty girl."

I studied the horizon over Lancaster, and the words came out before I knew I would say them. "I can't do it," I said. I turned to look, to see his reaction.

He kept his gaze straight ahead. He asked if there was someone else.

"What? No," I said. I gestured to him and to me, certain now. "I just think it shouldn't be this hard."

What I really meant, though I didn't know it, was that it shouldn't be this easy — the way a trap door gives away on a gallows scaffolding.

Deep down, I preferred romantic interests to be distant enough to seem fictional, like guys I met in France with whom I could flirt but not converse. They didn't disturb my butterflies.

When Graham drove away in his red Volkswagen hatchback, I knew I was supposed to chase the car, bang on the windows. But instead, I stood in the road and watched him go, like the Final Girl — like I'd survived something. I didn't know that I wouldn't see him again, that he would exist only as a text, an email, an image of a fireman in navy that was there when I closed my eyes, so close that his breath rustled my hair, nor that we would each find long-term relationships eventually with others, nor that it would take years longer for me than for him.

What I did understand, albeit without language, was that, okay, this situation wasn't quite *j'ai tout perdu*. I have lost everything. But still. I had, perhaps, stolen my own leeks.

In the Nest / Annie Dawid

Finalist Geminga 2024

The Morning After You Passed

Alfie White

Geminga 2024 Best of Fiction

I changed the sheets, washed, put on deodorant, tried to read and eventually did; I turned on the news, saw that life carries on, looked outside and saw it there too; I watched an insect climb my bedroom wall and blew on it to make it fly, but it just fell down, down, down the crevice of my bed into that unreachable darkness; I prayed to a God that it found you there, that it carried a bit of my breath with it, a faint breeze lifting a stray hair of yours, reminding you, reminding you, of I don't know.

Dear Susan, I Am Your Antony — Emily D.

Rosa Lane

Geminga 2024 Best of Poetry

Wind-driven, I'm off
to Alexandria, torqued,
compassed *mare nostrum* —
keel, ribs, tongues' hardwood, cockled
beguiled, you sway me steady.

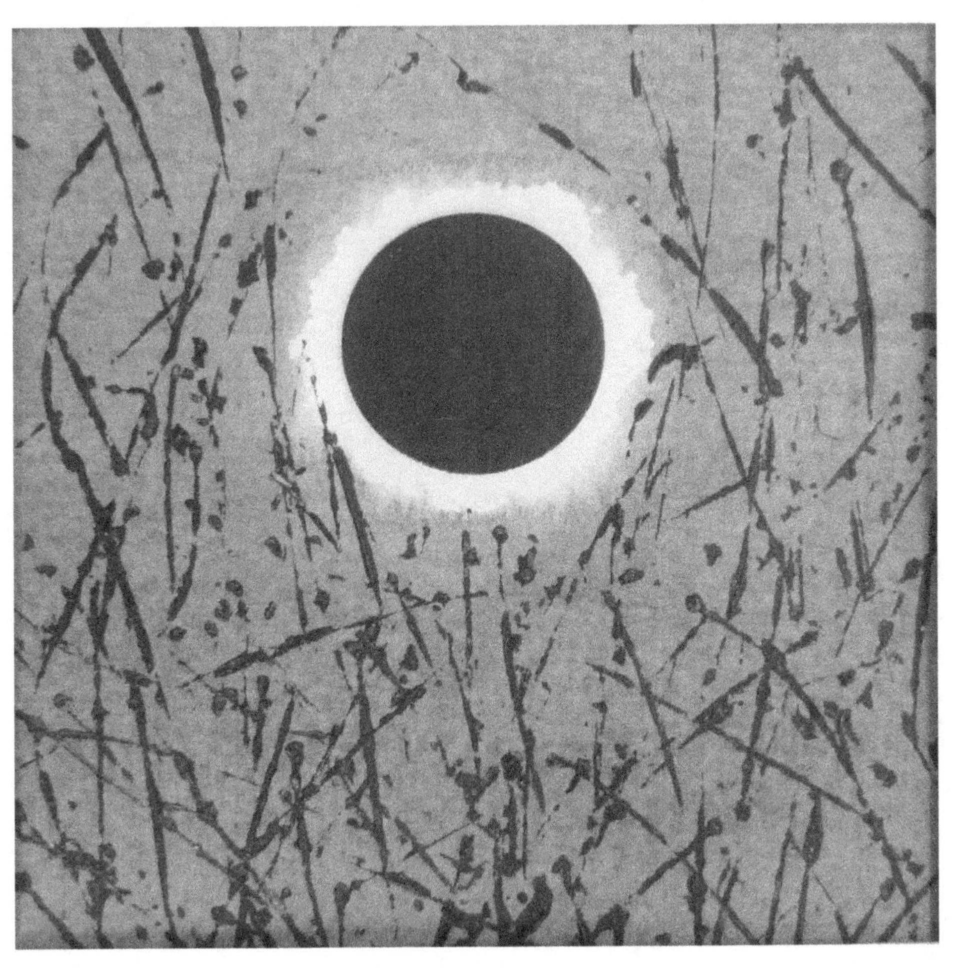

Don't Look Up / Pamela Viggiani

Geminga 2024 Winner

Eclipse

David Landau

Rigel 2024 Finalist

It's hot. I get out of bed. I go over and crack the window still half-asleep, stubbing my toe on the cardboard box by the dresser. *Fuck.* I look around the room at all the other boxes. Most of them already chock full. The rest still waiting for the last of things.

Funny how you forget.

I stand there, looking through the blind slats. There's a big moon coming up over my neighbor's house. No sooner does it crest the roofline, its beam casts my backyard in this eerie glow, like some searchlight after finding its target.

I scissor the blinds open wider with two fingers and lean in closer. My toe hurts. I watch everything.

Everything that's still there, that is.

The chaise lounges, set side by side in the middle of the lawn. The wilting potted plants on the terra-cotta tile. The diving board with its broken spring. *Never did get that fixed, they'll dock us for that.* The grill grate leaning up against the Weber BBQ legs, jail-like. And imagine all the creepy-crawlies that come out at night, slipping through the bars, and going on the lam. The light sconces mounted on the stucco siding. The metal ones with the moon and star cutouts we bought at the little stand in Tuscany in the rain. *I wonder if we can take those with us.* And just beneath, the kinked-up hose. *They can have that.* I wish I was a bug.

I look back at the digital clock on the nightstand. Just shy of 3:00 a.m. It's then I remember reading about the eclipse that's supposed to happen about now. My wife's sleeping, breathing quietly. Her hair limp in the humidity. And nightgown damp against her breasts in the glow of the clock.

I watch a moment. I can just make out a bead of sweat snaking down her throat. I wait for her to stir. And when she doesn't stir, I look out at the chaise lounges again. I wipe some of my own sweat off my face. And think to myself. I think, *Wouldn't it be funny . . . ?*

Then I do it.

I slip off my pajamas and tiptoe out the French doors — well, tiptoe as best I can on account my big one still's sore — and go lay on the chaise. I angle the back down on its lowest rung. Look up at the moon. And wait for something to happen.

And I have to tell you, it feels nice lying there, a slight breeze cooling my body. Creeping in and around all the crevices. Real peaceful too. Except for the vinyl webbed strapping a bit scratchy on my bare bum. Mostly it feels strange. I mean, I've been in this house thirty years and never once did I ever get the gumption to go outside at three o'clock in the morning and lie butt naked on a chaise.

I lie there for some time. I listen for the crickets. I watch the moon — a tiny piece of it is missing now. The sky's turning a strange color. I wonder what the odds are of the International Space Station passing right overhead at this exact moment. *Should I cover up?*

I think of the guy who strapped a bunch of helium balloons to his lawn chair and took off and was spotted miles high by a passing 737. I think he kept his clothes on. I wonder if my backside is all crosshatched from the vinyl strapping. I wish I had some balloons.

Then there's this noise coming from the side of the house. Where we keep the trash cans. Must be a raccoon, I'm sure of it. A whole family of them's moved in. And escrow hasn't even closed yet. I think to myself, *That's funny*. But who cares, really. It's somebody else's problem now. So is that old can. Been trying to get rid of it, like forever now. Put it out next to the rest of those fancy plastic containers the city gave us. But the garbagemen never take it. I mean, think about it . . . how does one throw out a trash can anyway?

And just when I am thinking about that, like it's one of the great mysteries of the universe, I see this lone star. I try to guess which one it is. I go through all the obvious names I know: Sirius, Arcturus, Vega, Capella, Betelgeuse. Then I wonder who names the stars in the first place. And if you tried to name all the stars, how far would you get before you ran out of names? I think how great a name Theodosia would be for a star. That's my wife's name, Theodosia. I look over at her through the crack I left in the French doors. And tell myself to ask her in the morning if I can borrow her name for a star. *It would have to be a noble star, though, to be called that.*

The moon's half-gone now. The sky's getting darker. I can see more stars.

Just then the pool pump shuts off. Everything goes quiet. I can hear myself breathing. I can hear my own heartbeat. I wonder, if you were up in space high enough, could you hear the moon and planets go by?

I wish our son was here. I wish our dog hadn't died. I wish we didn't have to sell the house.

I wish, I wish I could wield a giant broom and sweep all the scattered stars like so much dust into a pile in some far corner of the universe. And throw them out with the trash, for all the good they do sometimes.

It's then I hear another noise. But it isn't a raccoon this time. I look, and there's Theodosia walking across the lawn. She comes up, lifting a strap off her shoulder with the slip of a finger. Then the other. Gets that look in her eye and starts to slink out of her nightgown. But all it does is stick to her skin from the humidity. Finally, she pulls it off, dropping it at her feet. And lies down on the chaise beside me.

"Couldn't sleep?" she says.

"Ran out of sheep. Switched to stars."

She smiles. Looks back at the house. Then squeezes my hand.

"It's time."

"No, it's not. It's money. The lack of it, that is."

"I'd rather lack money than time with you." She looks around the yard. "God, that old diving board. Remember when Johnny did the backflip the first time? How old was he, four maybe? You were so proud."

"Then I tried."

"Yes, you did. And split your chin on the end of the board. Blood everywhere."

"It was fun, though."

"And remember how you used to whack the avocados off the tree with the pool net?"

"Wish we still had that tree so we could sell 'em, they were so big. We'd make a fortune."

"And remember when we lost power that time, and it was Johnny's birthday party, and you cooked the frozen pizzas on the BBQ?"

"I was just being sensible."

"God, they tasted awful."

"When we first met, you said you were attracted to the strong, sensible type."

"I think that was strong, *sensitive* type."

"Well, whatever. That was long ago and far away." I then turn toward her, her nipples erect in the humid night. "We could mess around . . . ."

"Yes, we could. Or, on second thought, we could just be."

"I still got it in me, you know."

"Yes, you do." She smiles, then looks deep into the night. "By the way, it wouldn't work."

"What wouldn't work?"

"All those stars you'd sweep into some far corner of the sky. They'd just create a giant sun piled up like that, and light up the whole universe."

"What?"

"You were talking out loud. That's what woke me."

"Oh, I do that. Don't I?"

"Yes, you do."

I look up, way up, trying to see what she's seeing.

"I've loved this old house."

"As have I."

I feel for Theodosia's hand and find it.

"Remind me to ask you something in the morning."

And with the moonlight now all but gone, we lie naked together under the star-strewn sky. Just touching.

Getting the last of it before the movers come.

The Older Man

Alan Sincic

Rigel 2024 Finalist

Respect the older man. When he was a baby they gathered around him. Respect the older man. He ate his vegetables. There is a turn to his ankle where the polio missed him. The falling safe missed but he helped them count the money, the great war missed but he helped them stack the bodies respect the older man. The mad dog missed him and the trolley car swerving, the invisible contagion on the rim of the drinking glass and the assassin's dinner invitation and the suicide's masterful logic and the mad accidental excitement of the ten-year binge. Hundreds are dying as he eats his breakfast. He missed, he was missed, missed the purge and the spoiled tuna salad, the letter bomb and the sucker punch and the iridescent blue of the shark infested waters. He wipes his mouth and a thousand fall. Respect the older man.

He did not land on the silver screen and there are no shots of his smooth young cheeks and respect — a million times he has wiped his face and still it has not left him.

Respect, respect the — it is his belief that the woman still remembers the look of his thighs, the children still remember where their bodies began. Do not break the legs of the older man. His eyes are his only ornament. The hairs of his head have left of their own accord, he wears the skull of his head with pride, he points but his arms go off in a different direction but not break the arms of the older man, his arms are the arms of a compass and they point to the places where he's been and they point the way they pointed when he was a baby, and they gathered and they asked him what he wanted and in every direction is the direction that he pointed.

Respect the older man, he is going where his body cannot go, he is an acrobat, he is practicing a trick, he is thinking of a stunt, his body he forgets and he gathers it in pieces when he stands. Respect the older man he is a daring piece of furniture, he folds his bones like a broken umbrella, his legs are the legs of an elegant chair, his arm is a clock, is a clock, and he goes by the blood in his wrist. He calculates the steps to the door, the weight of his head, the size of the earth.

Respect the older man. He stands in his roots, he is no longer green, it is hard to remove him. He cannot be retrieved. He stands in his roots, he is waiting for fire, he cannot be retrieved.

He has memorized the sun in the lines of his face and the moon in the whites of his bones. Respect the older man.

He shrinks in his clothes like a man underwater, a slow-motion man in a big diving suit, he lives at the bottom of a thousand feet of water and he cannot be recognized by his high school photo and his record is clean and he cannot be arrested and he moves too slowly to be noticed by the police. Respect the older man.

When he was born he was shot out of a cannon and the crowd rose and cheered like their seats as well were wired with shot and out into the naked air he went a good trick but it took too long and now the crowd has gone home, the tent packed away, a garden planted in the sawdust ring and a vine of tomatoes growing up the face of the net, and still he sails out through the air looking back at the cannon's mouth and wondering how he ever fit, his ass to the stars and the smoke rising up from his neighbors bright homes like warm little factories spreading farther and farther beneath him.

Respect the older man, do not deny the older man, the falling safe missed and he helped them count the money, the great war missed and he helped them stack the bodies, the mad dog missed and the trolley car swerving, the purge and the tuna and the bomb and the punch and the iridescent blue of the shark infested waters and do not deny the older man. He looks at the flesh on your soft pink arm, he wipes his mouth and a thousand fall.

Stand in the tower of your own hard body and wait for the visit of the older man, respect him, respect him, become an invitation, clasp your bones to the bole of your heart and wait for the visit of the older man. Respect the older man, wait for the older man, do not hurry the older man he is a long-time traveler, he is a marathon, he is a killer, he keeps you waiting the whole of your lifetime then at last he is here. Respect the older man. Stand in his bones and look out of his eyes. Respect the older man.

Disturbances

Lenora Steele

Rigel 2024 Best of Poetry

The rocks in our gardens, of which there are quite
a number, we chose; all of them
over the years on drives and jaunts to
beaches and streams, to fields and forests.
Every one picked for its particular shape or color
or history. At one time we
could tell you where each was found,
we were always finding them. These days the heft
has grown heftier; we don't bring so many home anymore.
We have taken to collecting stones though. Small white stones, and filling
our inexhaustible pockets with the little kernels of time.

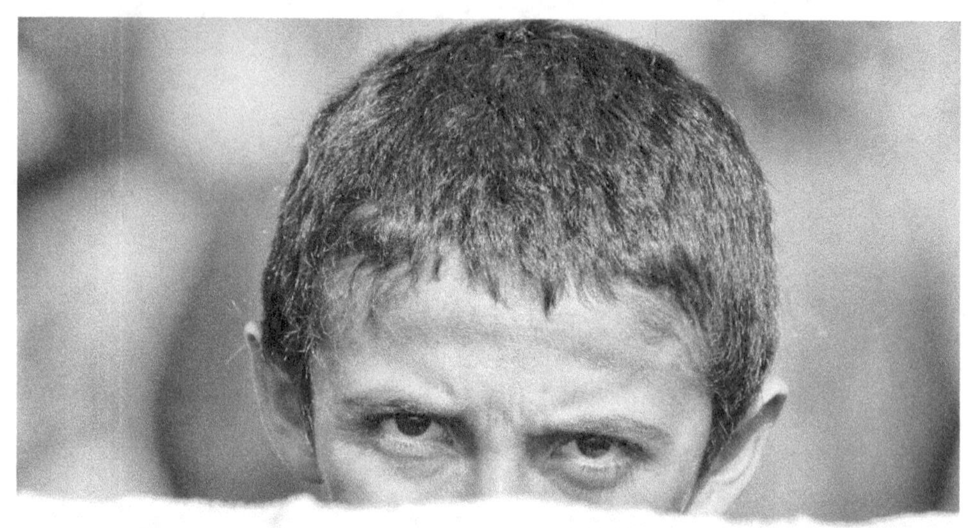

Guardian, On the Road to Mt. Nemrud — Turkiye, 2011

/ William Lewis Winston

Rigel 2024 Best of Art

The Key Is to Keep Saying Sorry

Adrian Fleur

Rigel 2024 Best of Fiction

She had blue strands twisted in her braids, and white and pale yellow and grey. She had a head chock full of them, curling down around her neck, tightly wound and tied up neatly at each end. I could close my eyes and still see the imprint of those twists being twisted, round and round by tired fingers at the taxi rank in town. We had spent a good six hours waiting for her hair to get done, guzzling Cokes and gnawing on *biltong* in the sun. My best friend, the girl with the colorful braids in a purple tutu and striped stockings who was now yelling *Drink!* in the club. It was a Thursday night and we were underage, yelling over Seether while clinking together our too-sweet Bacardi Breezers.

Drink! I'd never been a good drinker: always too full too quickly, too tired, hungover before the booze could hit me sideways, aching for bed long before the lights came on and we were shooed away home. *Drink! Drink so we can go talk to those boys!* I'd never been one for drinking, let alone drinking and talking — let alone talking to boys. I'd get by with smiles, with laughs, with lame high-fives. I had no jokes, no pleasantries; I had yet to grow an enticing personality. I was seventeen, remember. I didn't know any better, or how to live any differently.

I'm going to talk to him, to that one! Tim? His name is Tim. Or is it Nick? She was so drunk, I thought. More drunk than the night we'd pinched her mom's brandy and made a bonfire in her backyard and sang out of tune while playing guitar. She was more drunk than our most recent slumber party where some kid named Sky or Storm got rushed off to the ER to get her stomach pumped — and we all knew it had more to do with a bunch of teenage girls practicing kissing each other than with the alcohol percentage in cheap beer or wine coolers. She was even more drunk than that one terrible morning after we'd crashed a 21st the night before, and some older girl taught us about hair of the dog and made us down leftover milk stout for breakfast. She was so drunk, and I knew it was going to be a bad time, but I didn't have the foresight to stop her or fix things or take us home. I was seventeen, remember, and so she dragged us over to Nick and his friends and planted us square in front of them. And I saw the glint in his green eyes, I took note, I faltered, but then I straightened up and pushed away the moment. I tried to sound like an adult when I said to him, *Hey, Nick! How're you doing?*

Heeeey! It's you two! They watched us. They stared.

Great! Hi! We just wanted to say hi. That's why we came over here. Just to say hi.

Well, it's about time!

I should have said hi earlier, when we saw you. I just couldn't reach you. In the bar, you know? Anyway, my friend, well — you know each other, right?

That's me! She wobbled on her feet.

She wanted to say hi too, I guess. I could feel embarrassment growing on my cheeks.

Neat. Sweet. So how come you never say hi to me in school?

My friend nudged me in the ribs, and inwardly I groaned and rolled my eyes.

Don't I? Maybe it's because you're the grade above me. I'm not sure.

Oh, it's not that. I've seen you talking to Dax and those guys. I've seen you hanging around with Ray sometimes. It's not that. Maybe you're shy?

Again, the nudge in the ribs, the groan, the eye roll.

I don't know. Maybe it's that then. Anyway, bye!

And I hauled us both back to the tables in the far corner on the roof, back to my boyfriend and some other people we knew, and my best friend laughed deliriously and squealed, *He likes you! He likes you!*

And that's when Jeffrey flew up, demanding, *Who? Who likes you? Who?* And she thought it was a game, so she told him, *Nick! This guy from our school.* And then he punched me in the face.

I was seventeen, remember. I didn't know what you were supposed to do when your boyfriend punched you in a public place. So I just lay on the ground for a while. I felt lame as ever — as usual — I felt dumb and small and paralyzed. I guess those feelings blocked out the pain. And then all of our friends flew into a rage, yelling, throwing bottles, shoving each other and screaming at Jeffrey and then, at some point, I was pulled up. And my best friend kept saying, *I'm so sorry! I'm so sorry!* And Jeffrey was there, in the space where I stood, his face that I loved which in dreams so often became a demon, the glint in his green eyes the same one I'd seen so many times, that I thought I'd seen just minutes before in the eyes of a new boy, because all boys had that glint in their eye, didn't they? Didn't they? But Nick had never punched me before, pushed me into walls, pulled my hair or clawed at me, or swore at me and called me names. *Slut! Whore!* I can't remember them all now. I managed to say, at one point while Jeffrey was screaming at me, *I was just saying hey! I was talking to him for her.* But he always hated when I tried to explain. So he stopped screaming at me and pushed me away, but instead of going away, I fell back down to the ground onto my dumb body that never worked properly. I just fell down like the dumb seventeen-year-old I was, like Jeffrey always said I was, like that was all I knew how to be, because I was only seventeen — remember?

I'm so sorry, I'm so sorry! My best friend couldn't stop herself from crying and telling me she was sorry. I knew that same jingle, I used it all the time. *I'm so sorry, I'm so sorry.* She was so drunk, more drunk than I'd ever seen her. She couldn't stop telling everyone else she was sorry too. Our friends. Jeffrey. The big bouncers who came to take him away. *I'm so sorry.* And when I got up again she brought me water, but I didn't need it. By then I was sober. Every time she looked over she just cried harder. I told her I was fine. She told me she was sorry.

The bar owner came over. I'd never liked her and her stupid pigtails and her drawn-on eyebrows. I always ducked when she came too close, scared she'd I.D. us, call the cops and kick us out. Kill the shots, the vodka-sodas, the Bacardi Breezers. I guess that night I realized she was all right. She was one of those older women who knew it all, who thought she'd pass on some wisdom to us young chicks. She crouched down and told us about some prick she married back in the 90s, about how much time she wasted with him, about how she could have lived her life so differently — if only she'd known better. I didn't really get it (I was seventeen, remember). All I wanted was to go home and sleep off my hangover and wake up with my best friend so we could catch the number 10 bus to the beach, and buy ice creams that melted all over our skin as soon as we took them out from under the shade and into the blistering Durban sun, and then we'd give our change to the guys who slept in the space between the barriers and the sea, who made sand sculptures of elephants and dinosaurs and would even make us into sand mermaids if we gave them a sip of our ice teas or the dregs of our over-sauced Wimpy chips. All I wanted was to go back to earlier that day, that perfect day we had just lived with the sin of sugar and meat on our lips, when our butts were parked in camping chairs at the taxi rank while Mdu braided my best friend's hair from scratch, and we read each other's horoscopes and laughed at the back page of *Heat* magazine, at the pictures of the silly speech bubbles coming out of the mouths of our favorite celebrities.

All I wanted was simplicity. I didn't know how to live my life any differently. I was only seventeen, remember.

Proper Adults

Caitlyn Moony

Rigel 2024 Winner

It's Friday afternoon, and I am clipping away at my hydrangeas with the kind of meditative focus that comes with years of exhaustion and quietly swallowed injustices. Tom has told me to just leave them this weekend, considering all the incoming guests and commotion. He warned me the lawn would get all stomped on by everyone's heels and children. That I'd end up back at it on Sunday morning anyway. And he's right, of course. Maybe I should just pull them all out.

My long, perfectly manicured gravel drive, filled with its tiny, carefully selected little grey pebbles would have looked so beautiful with neat pink and white rose bushes. But the cliche of it would have killed me. I hate roses, thanks to my mother's drug-induced romanticism when the midwife had asked for a name.

"*Mom!*" I inhale sharply and start towards the front door where the yelling has emanated from, turning straight from my kneeling position and twisting my knee grotesquely as I stand. I wince with pain but dig the garden shears hard into my closed fist and breathe through it.

I have seen other mothers grow into a state of zenned-out tranquility, a languid laissez-faire as their kids morph from infants to toddlers, and toddlers to children. A "*so he's stuck another pen in his eye, that's why he's got two,*" kind of attitude that comes with surviving watching your offspring put themselves in the line of deathly peril on a moment-to-moment basis. Boy Moms. For the first three years of my mothering life, I was one. But as eagerly, as desperately as I had wanted to stay one those moms, my second child had been a girl, and with that the Zen had dissipated into the ether like cigarette smoke blown sneakily through a bathroom window.

I had waited patiently for that sense of confident ease, and the superior smile that came with it, to return. It never did. Every single bleat, whine, groan from my little girl, and my heartbeat races into high gear. It is the Boy Mom's job to let him be him. To let him make mistakes, and push boundaries, and ask for forgiveness rather than permission. The Boy Mom must shrug off her anxiety from her tense shoulders and "let boys be boys". That doesn't work for girls, though. It is the Girl Mom's job to push, to prod, to poke, and to protect. To point out flaws, and paths to flawlessness. It's a lot. A Girl Mom must embrace her anxiety, she must lean into it and let it consume her. It's a Girl Mom's job to feel, perpetually, like a failure.

"Mo-om!!" my lamb bleats again, slightly higher pitched this time.

I stride swiftly up the grassy slope that runs parallel to the drive towards the house, forcing my knee to take as much weight as the other. I refuse to be the kind of woman who hobbles. I will be old and grey with brittle bones and arthritic toes, and I will walk as I do now, even if it kills me.

Meegan stands leaning against the front door with a jutting out pubescent hip. She taps her bare wrist with the finger of her other hand and gives me one of her looks.

"Mother," she whines at me again, and I reach out to stroke the side of her freckled little face, relieved there doesn't seem to be any immediate life-threatening emergency; pissed off that I've screwed up my knee for no apparent reason. Of course, I could tell myself that next time I will ignore it and stay pruning my plants, because it's never, ever really anything urgent. But you can't do that, can you? You're not allowed, them's the rules. Child yells, mother runs. We're all just a bunch of Pavlov's dogs. And we're never allowed to talk about it lest we be, not a Boy Mom or a Girl Mom but, worst of all, a Bad Mom.

Meegan pulls away, flicking her long blond hair over one shoulder. Meegan has always been Tom's child, both physically and in their mutual flair for the dramatic. By fourteen, she is already almost taller than me, and slim and muscular. I am small and dark and, as Tom likes to phrase it, "juicy".

My youngest offspring will soon tower above me, casting a shadow over me, and still demand me to cut the crusts off her sandwiches.

"Mom, it's nearly two? Shouldn't you be getting things ready for tonight? Nothing is set out yet and guests will be arriving in like, three hours? It's stressing me out. And Stuart has been in the bathroom for like an hour!" She yells, this last part, for the benefit of her older brother, I assume. Her bottom lip juts out in a little pout, and I wonder where she learned that from. Certainly not from me.

"Alright, Meegan," I soothe. "I've just finished up in the garden, and we can start getting stuff ready here in the kitchen, ok? Do you want to help?"

I still feel like I've got little children sometimes. I'd had to grow up much quicker. Tom and I met while I was in school, married while I was still in university, moved into this old farmhouse that I inherited from my parents, and then had the kids. We both studied law, but it's just him practicing. I'm official hydrangea pruner and child wrangler.

"No, I need to get ready, obviously?" She looks at me like I've been knocked on the head with an idiot stick. That's why you need to get Stu out of the bathroom." I shudder to think what the kid has been up to in there for an hour.

Everyone said that when you have a second, the older one will eventually help out. Not at first, of course, not while they're still adapting to not being the only star anymore, but eventually. That never happened with Stu, though. He just never adapted. He still views Meegan as a little parasite that sucks everything away from him.

Meegan lurks behind me while I bang on the bathroom door. "Stuey, my love? Everything ok in there?" Silence.

"Honey, it's getting late, and we all need to start getting ready. Can you come and help me in the kitchen and give Meegan a chance to get in there, please?" There's a rush of water and then my pink-faced boy slinks out, shoving his shoulder hard into Meegan as he pushes past towards his room, making her squawk with indignance.

"I was in there for like ten minutes," he grumbles.

"Oh, please," Meegan rolls her eyes. "He wasn't," she says to me, conspiratorially. "And look what a mess he's made." There is water splashed all over the floor and I grab a towel from the rail, shuffling it under my feet as if I am some fifties shimmying housewife.

"Ok, your turn to get in there," I smile at her and unsuccessfully try to caress her cheek again.

"But I need to eat something first?"

We stare at each other and for a moment, I don't know how to respond. I want to ask why she interrupted my gardening to yank poor Stu out of the bathroom if she wasn't even in a hurry to get in there. I want to ask why she hasn't made herself a sandwich. I want to ask why she couldn't have asked her father to help with any of this.

But I really don't want to get into a fight right now; it'll just delay everything, and I honestly don't think I have it in me this afternoon. If I was *my* mother, I would have asked her if she really thought eating something was a good idea. I would have looked her up and down while I asked, waiting for her face to crumple in insecurity. I would have told her the party was no place for little children, so if she wanted to attend, she was going to have to grow up, and grow up fast. But I'm not my mother.

She's Undone / GJ Gillespie

Inception 2024 Finalist

Reflection in Orange / Robin Young

Inception 2024 Finalist

My Glittering City / Heather P. Shreve

Inception 2024 Finalist

Your Body is Real / Anna Troxell

Inception 2024 Finalist

Ginger Cake

Indyana Horobin

Inception 2024 Best of Creative Nonfiction

I watch my grandfather hold his mug of coffee. He inhales through his nose before he sips. I do too. Smelling the roast before tasting. I'm recording us. My phone set down on the table, a microphone plugged in. I'm recording because I'm writing this. These words, this book. I've planned time in the week with him and my grandmother. I'm going to take their stories. I'm going to make them live in text. I'm going to keep them alive with words.

Rodney's first positive memory of life is being handed a slice of ginger cake with lemon icing. He's seven years old. His ribs protrude, skin wrapping thin over the bones, eyes deep set in a face missing baby fat. Malnourishment makes him seem younger. Rod lives on the Wombarra coastline. He doesn't know it yet but when he gets home, his father will beat him. Jack Horobin, doesn't want Rodney to have anything nice. Rod was born into a family of ten, he was the sixth, and when he arrived things were already . . . pretty fucking bad. His father–drinking and bashing his mother every night; his mother–a couple years into a full-blown psychotic episode. They both do things to Rodney that stick in his memory, hot tar on gravel, napalm, boiling; angry and permanently there. His parents scream at him to stop crying, to stop talking, to not be seen or heard, to have not existed in the first place.

Eulogistic Texts to My Dead Girlfriend as a Timeline of Grief

Kyo Lee

Inception 2024 Best of Fiction

April 15 11:43 PM

hey

how're u

me? thanks for asking.

the past three months have swallowed me and severed me into pieces. winter was beautiful this year. one day I woke up to a world blanketed with snow, sky and ground holding each other so tight they appeared to merge under the violet dawn air, and when I fell back asleep, I dreamt that your blood was staining the snow a terrible red.

I woke up to the clattering of my teeth. it was as if my skull was shaking from the cold, as if I could feel your blood sticking to me. I turned on the shower and sat on the bathtub shivering but this reminded me of the nights, when we were children, how we'd paint each other's nails in the same tub. bare skin of my shin sliding against yours under the blanket, our legs shifting around so more of ourselves could touch each other, our naive bodies seeking what they wanted as we, above the blanket, said nothing. I would've continued to say nothing if you were alive.

anyway. the reason i'm messaging you is that you've returned to life. there's this rat who i met in the apartment dumpster & everyday he convinces me that he is you. he has narrow black eyes bulging out of him, like flowers ready to bloom, and he has this charm and charisma. i sometimes mistake him for you. resurrection is not a glorious matter. you would know.

Comfort / JC Chen Henderson

Inception 2024 Best of Art

THE BUDDHA TRAIN

STEPHEN POLICOFF

INCEPTION 2024 BEST OF NOVEL

The damn phone would not stop ringing.

After the first call I knew there would be more. Journalists have some universal hook-up; it's like when one monkey learns a new skill and suddenly the whole clan can slit a gourd in half with a sharpened stone. I couldn't answer most of their questions. And those I could answer I did not answer.

Even now, I do not know how he came to be where he was when it happened and certainly I do not know — do not care, *do not care* — why his once-bright star fell so precipitously.

Here is what I do know: Gabriel Bish, famous/infamous creator of theater epics, prince of the avant-garde, appears to have died in the first days of the year 2000, under circumstances far removed from the bohemian splendor in which he had once lived. The cause? *A crude explosive device*, according to Connecticut State Troopers; *a highly sophisticated detonation*, according to the **Hartford Courant**.

Terrorism? Perhaps. He enraged many political partisans who sought his attention. An act of revenge by someone whose life he damaged? Possibly. But there are so many candidates. Where would one even start?

Everyone else is astonished. I may be too tired of refusing to think about him to be in the least surprised by his horrible death.

I suppose I shouldn't blame them for tracking me down. But I do. In the years since Gabriel Bish ruined my life, I've felt vaguely safe up here in Ulster County.

Sea Horse: An Ode

G.R. Kramer

Inception 2024 Winner

I arose with the squat rouge heart
of the newbirthed sun and saw
on the shore the filly, pale,
riderless, feral horse
in shoaling waves,

His T-shirt and Mine

Milo Harvey

Goldilocks Zone 2024 Finalist

There's a certain weight that grows within your chest when your cousin appears wearing the image of an AR-15 within the silhouette of Texas on his heather gray T-Shirt and for months all you can think of is dying and you slowly become hardened by it and a fear and a pain cements there like a grit in the joints between your bones and you clench your teeth and you've noticed your gums bleeding and you taste it in your mouth like iron and you turn cold and sad and just oh so exhausted from watching the threads grow longer and the bottom feeders killing each other and the blood fills the tank and your other cousin tells you what your great-aunt said about you last summer and how she argued and said she'd never try to understand and didn't care to anyway and after a while you just stopped even fighting it and when you float through the store like a specter you feel a small, welcome sense of relief because the employee who helped you had a layer beneath his voice that you recognize and as you trudge out into the baking, humid parking lot you think of hot, hot red, a beautiful flower you will only see once, deep red petals blooming through the thin white cotton of your T-Shirt, expanding slowly, steadily outwards and all you can do is watch and think oh how beautiful it is, the color red, and you think about the man in the parking lot killing you, or the man at the concert in the square, and you think about your cousin killing you and on the cusp of every thought, in every breath of consciousness, you glimpse into the cool glass of fear and stare into the scared eyes of your own mortality, the gentle breaths you take, so easily halted and you wonder how a heart can keep beating when such a tiredness overwhelms you, but not the kind of tiredness that dissipates into sleep, but the kind that aches your bones and curses you and brings you to your knees to cry "Oh God, why, why must I watch this all happen, how am I supposed to eat something that never goes down, swallow when it's impossible to chew" but you sleep as much as you can and you hope that the countless nights will make it waver and every morning you eat your instant oatmeal, stirring in the boiling water but leaving it runny and you forget about it, but never for very long. No, never for very long.

Maybe Both

Jordan Nishkian

Goldilocks Zone 2024 Finalist

The equipment in this room looks different than the one from last month, even though Dr. Lin made the procedures sound similar.

This one is different. This one comes with a cauterizer, a vacuum, a waiver, and Nurse Daisy telling me it could make it harder to carry a pregnancy to term.

Until I heal from this, that makes sense.

"Forever," she corrects.

The wax paper crinkles under my shifting hips. Apparently, you can only get almost-cancer so many times before your cervix stops letting you have babies.

Do I even want babies?

I start to cry.

I guess so.

Nurse Daisy says the doctor will explain everything to me before the procedure, which seems out of order to me. She says I don't have to sign yet.

I wasn't thinking of ending things when I got curious about the little locked box under my ex's side of the bed. I knew about it for years, but the morning he left for a week-long trip, I felt the urge to look at it. Crisp, finger-sized streaks disrupted the lid's thick layer of dust the way knowing this disrupted my day. A combination lock from a suitcase was all that stood between me and what I already knew.

I glide my name over the waiver's empty line. This is where I let the universe decide, hoping it'll intervene via dead pen, or maybe something more dramatic like a fire alarm or a not-so-serious earthquake. Despite the clinic's location between two fault lines (I checked), divine intervention kept to herself. The ink flowed smoothly onto the paper.

I relinquish the clipboard, the documents, and my cervical cells to Nurse Daisy, who looks a little bad for seeing me crack — I'm not as good at not-crying in a doctor's office as I am at not-crying at a funeral — but takes what I offer and tells me to relax till she comes back.

There are a lot of things to like about Nurse Daisy: that she doesn't treat me preciously, that her nails are always pink, but what I like most right now is that she doesn't ask me if I'm sure.

Of course I'm not sure, but I made the appointment, searched for parking for fifteen minutes, put on the single-ply gown, and tucked my underwear into a stack of performatively folded clothes on a chair. What am I supposed to do? Let myself get worse?

I fail at not-looking at the equipment the way I fail at not-crying. What awaited me on the metal tray looked anything but delicate. These were the things I wanted preciousness from — for the silver nitrate to be stored in crystal, for the speculum to be wrapped in pastel silicon, for the stirrups to be heated and cushioned while the rustling sanitary paper whispers encouragement. I try lying down in case it has anything to tell me, but all it gives is an untranslatable crackle.

Seven days before he realized I left him (AKA: "Lockbox Day"), I called out of work and spent the morning trying different lock combinations and searching for the key. I spent the daylight combing through hoarded, miscellaneous papers spread over his desk, shoved into drawers, and tucked between old DVDs and magazines. I checked my phone every twenty minutes — when he texted me in the late afternoon, I didn't respond. (My therapist says I avoid anger by seeking power.

She also says I restrict myself from my emotions. I tell her I cry all the time.

"But what do you feel?"

Nothing.)

I ease myself off the examination table and onto the linoleum, trying to decipher the paper's static response. The woo-woo part of me says it's radio static, but I'm not tuned into the right station to receive the message (the woo-woo part of me often makes the situation my fault), while the mm-hmm part of me says to stop making something out of nothing (it also makes the situation my fault). I help myself to a tissue to clean my teary face and blow my nose, glad I didn't have time for makeup this morning.

I wipe my eyes greedily and move to the wall of posters and brochures. There's a year-old printout about insurance updates, and beneath it, a flier with the new esthetician sticking a needle into Nurse Daisy's forehead. Something about a women's health clinic offering Botox felt like it could either be sexist or empowering. (I'm tempted to throw my tissue into the red biohazard disposal.) Maybe neither, maybe both.

I didn't find the key on Lockbox Day, but I found a hotel parking pass. I called the Sonata Inn at 4 p.m., but Mike at the front desk said he couldn't share protected information. I called the Sonata Inn again at 2 a.m. This time, a bored Bernice was more than happy to help (I think about her sometimes) and reported that his license plate was connected to a string of one-night reservations made under a name that frequented his phone screen.

I'm straightening a stack of pamphlets when Dr. Lin knocks and walks into the room with Nurse Daisy. There's a lot to like about her — Dr. Lin — the way her fuchsia pants and floral blouse billow out of her white coat, the way she sits with me and draws a bunch of circles and lines on the back of my chart to explain the procedure, the way she (later) narrates what she's doing from between my knees, even though she uses words I don't like: "cough," "cut," "cauterize."

The four Cs of diamonds come to mind (which I only know about because of my close relationship with delusion). I try to think of the fourth C of gynecology.

I wince at the astringent smell of vinegar and burning flesh (my burning flesh).

Cry could work.

After the breakup, I drove to the beach in the middle of the night, parked across from my college apartment, and walked down the ramp next to the pier, sliding out of my shoes before stepping off the concrete (I tend to go there when things end — books, relationships, lives). The sky was black with the new moon, smattered with faint stars, the sand chilled the tender skin between my toes, the waves and the wind were louder than my thoughts. After walking along the shoreline to the highest dune, I unclenched my jacket from my body and dropped it, along with my shoes, my shirt, and my jeans, beside my cold feet.

"Are you doing okay?"

No, but I nod. Chills unfurl over my skin; I stare at the pocked ceiling tiles. The pain-seeking part of me is piqued when Dr. Lin says, "Good job." (It doesn't react to praise the way it normally does when my legs are open. I want to lose that part of me.)

"Almost done," Dr. Lin says. "You still have plenty of cervix left."

The fourth C: "congratulations/condolences." My eyes travel to the bulletin board full of baby photos on the wall. Dozens of baby eyes watch me get slashed and burned.

My feet flew across the beach faster than my thoughts could keep up. I had the urge to do this for almost a decade (to plunge into the black, bitter water, piercing the sea foam and wetting my head, blending into the abyssal horizon). I ran against the push of the waves and followed their ebbing, arms cradled, eyes happy and burning. It was frigid. It was brief. It was mine — it was my favorite thing I'd ever done.

The night of the procedure, the rain convinces me to get the lockbox from the garage. It has a thin layer of dust on top, which started collecting a few months ago when I moved into my friend's house. Leah's house has an attic for storage, two bathrooms, and a backyard that we've become extra-enamored with (a ring of mushrooms appeared one day on the lawn). The glass door fogs as I look at it from the living room.

When Dr. Lin finished up and my knees fell together, she flipped a series of switches to turn off the machine. "You did great. I'll see you in four weeks to make sure you've healed completely," she said, discarding her gloves. I tried to ignore the black smears on the fingers before they disappeared into the trash. "Until then, no sex, no tampons, no baths, no swimming."

To punctuate this, Nurse Daisy pulled a printed list of restrictions from a folder and placed it on the counter next to a bulky pad. The burning smell lingered.

"Expect some cramping, and you'll want to use pads for the next few weeks; it'll be normal to see black stains. It's from the medicine."

I want nothing more than to fall into the midnight Pacific and get tumbled and scrubbed over jagged beds of broken rocks and shells (coquina — that's what that's called), then let the water salt each new wound. Again with the pain-seeking.

"Are you ok?"

No. I nodded, betrayed by welled-up eyes. Dr. Lin rubbed my knee. Nurse Daisy set down an extra pad. "Take your time," the doctor said before leaving.

I choked out a thank you, competing with the sound of the closing door.

A chill seeps through my shirt as I close the sliding glass door behind me, place the lockbox onto Leah's patio chair, and leave my slippers and jeans next to the legs.

Rain pelts my head and clings to my body while I cross over the field mushrooms to sit in the center of the fairy ring, imagining that my body could sink into the ground, the nape of my neck held by the soft edge of earth and bluegrass, bathing in its round, muddy mouth until the elves and pixies find me. (I want so badly to be swallowed — for my limbs and phalanges to root and branch and join the ring's mycelium network — sentience without a body.)

When Leah enters the yard, I'm curled in a fetal position, facing the light pouring out from the living room.

Can you see me?

"What are you doing?" she asks, lowering a trash bag and shutting the sliding door behind her.

This is supposed to make me invisible.

"That's a good way to upset the fairies," she says, waiting for my reaction (I have none). I pick dirt out from under my fingernails.

She watches me like I'm a maybe-dead possum on the side of the road. A halo of breath swells around her face before she pulls up her hood and moves the chair onto the lawn to join me, placing the lockbox on her lap as she takes a seat with crisscrossed legs.

"So, whatcha doing?"

I think this is as close as I can get to a bath for a while.

Maybe I'm not white enough for the fairy circle to work (the DNA test said I was 20%), but Leah's Irish. I'm tempted to ask her to try it.

"If you want a bath, we can just stick you in it upside-down." A dry smile crosses Leah's face while she fishes her favorite necklace out of her jacket pocket. "Can you get this?"

I sit up to catch the tangled chain, which ripples over the heart-shaped pendant in my muddy, concave palm. My nails set to work, trying to release the knot.

I'm about to consider that upside-down bath, then I remember that grief is stored in the hips, and as a woman, my hips are bowl-shaped — who knows how much is in there? Where would it go if I tip over? Maybe it'd put less pressure on my wounded cervix.

Leah leans an elbow on a rusted armrest. The rain drums on the lid of the box.

I worry sometimes I'm a fixer when I want to be a healer.

"Explains your relationship."

With my ex.

"With yourself."

Ow.

The rain falls in fat drops but only a few hit my face. The woo-woo part of me thinks I should be collecting it.

"I'm more of a fixer, it's not a bad thing," Leah says. "All those doctors and surgeons I had to see were more like fixers too."

I think about Dr. Lin.

"Do you think she's a healer?"

She has a bunch of awards in the hallway, so maybe both.

Does cutting out flesh count as healing? (My busy hands react to another wave of cramps.) Maybe neither.

"How many healers do you know?" she asks.

My mom is a chronic fixer. The rest — my grandmothers, my aunts — were neither. They were helpers, caregivers, young souls. The only person who claimed to be a healer was my ex's mother, although I'm not sure it's healing if she deals the damage in the first place. She was desperate to be one though, which might count for something.

"I think you're a healer in survival mode. There's nothing wrong with it."

I spent so much time trying to fix him.

"You were just trying to help."

The chain's knot starts to give. I push away the memories of asking what I could do to fix things. A worm wriggles out of the soil beneath my knee.

"You gave him the space, means, and time to do it; he just wouldn't get better. That's not on you. People don't get better all the time."

I pull the last of the tangled links apart and hand back the necklace, which she puts on in a practiced movement.

"K." The chair creaks when she stands, lockbox in hand. "Time to return the favor."

Leah examines the small box as she steps onto the patio, tosses it onto the concrete, and (in an equally practiced movement) drives the heel of her boot onto the hinges.

The raindrops sound different when they hit the bent metal as Leah walks the broken box back to me. Holding it over my lap, I curl my fingers under the new spaces of the lid and pull, revealing a scatter of fortune cookie slips, a blue poker chip, a Baskin Robbins gift card, and a corroded AA battery. I cover it all with a wail my chest thought it would die holding. The box drops onto the grass under the weight of my screams and curses and sobs, and now I know where the grief goes when I'm put upside-down.

My fingers loosen their grips from the dirt. The tears mix with rainwater, and — despite the cold — my shaking subsides. I look over to Leah, who's smiling.

"How do you feel?"

I let out a tired breath. "Better."

We sit in rain-fallen silence, holding the moment.

"Want me to throw that away for you?" she motions her head toward the garbage bag by the door. "I'm taking the trash out anyway."

I nod, reaching to pick up the box and its spilled contents.

"I got it," she waves me away. "Go get some coffee started."

I look skyward as I push myself up — face welcoming the warm patter, toes sinking into the lawn.

At the Edge of Things

William Lewis Winston

Goldilocks Zone 2024 Finalist

And here, in my skin, standing
at the sink and easing into the mirror,
and feeling the warmth of the day still in
the half-note wedge of fall that plays
through the blinds and spreads itself
on every surface waiting in its path,
I think, again, I have begun to lose my sight,
at least the focus it once held around the edges.

For as I move in close and just
tilt my head a guess or so to inspect
the sparse white stubble that needs
bordering along my jaw and below
the shifting sandy banks of my cheeks,
it is all a blur, a cautious breathing of
the light there — not too alarming, mind you,
for I have noticed it before in other untold stories.

But this autumn evening
I am out of comfort with aloneness,
and wonder how it might feel to
descend the back stairway to
the basement and from there to

reach for the short door and duck, as always,
so as not to hurt my head, into the garage,
and which tool I might finally choose.

Lucky Stones

Christy O'Callaghan

Goldilocks Zone 2024 Best of Fiction

Year, 1955

(Found materials in bold from "The Good Wife's Guide" from *Housekeeping Monthly* May 1955)

Have dinner ready.

She stripped off the soaked navy-blue canvas sneakers, cigarette pants and blouse, the Kelly green windbreaker, white socks, panties, and bra, dumping them in a pile on the steps by the kitchen door. Her shivering body naked in the spring air made brisk and foggy by the ocean. Scandalous thoughts had, on occasion, run through her head about walking around disrobed, letting the summer sun caress her stomach and breasts. The neighbors were too far away to see her. But this wasn't how she imagined it. The sodden pile of clothes waited as she wrung each article as best she could over the grass. Clapping the sneakers together, breaking loose the sand, tiny rocks, and mud. Debris sticking to her pale, damp skin.

The pile tucked in her arms, she made her way through the kitchen, relieved she'd already cleaned up her lunch of cucumber slices and onion soup. No one else was in the big, empty house, but she walked as quietly as possible so as not to raise awareness about what she'd done. Some things need to be kept secret. Once inside the bathroom with the door closed, she filled the sink with water and Woolite and soaked the clothes. She then turned on the hot tap in the shower. Each drop stung while it washed away the salt and the scent of seaweed.

Still shivering, she took a long swallow of her husband's Scotch. Dry, unblinking eyes barely registered the well-rehearsed movements of preparing his favorite meal until her heel pressed down onto something hard. She picked up the small gray stone with a perfect white ring around it. The lucky stone she'd clutched while walking into the drink.

Prepare yourself.

With dinner in the oven, she lay down on top of the bed, covering her numb body with a creamy white knit blanket. The freezing May ocean left her skin stinging, red, and itchy. Curled into a ball, she inhaled the scent of the wool afghan her Gran knitted as a wedding gift, each stitch filled with her hopes for a happy life full of love and babies. The small lucky stone pressed between her icy hand and the space below her belly button. Images of mossy green, apple blossoms bursting open, nests full of eggs, and bees with legs covered in yellow pollen played behind her closed lids. The doctor told her she must banish all negative thoughts and only make room for Life in order to grow a baby. If there was no baby, it was her fault for not wanting it enough, not wishing it enough.

She wouldn't tell the doctor about this afternoon and how the waves had beckoned her to join them. Calling as they hissed against the beach, shifting the stones with each lap. They seemed to understand how exhausted she was. They promised rest and peace.

The second alarm clock, closed away in her bedside drawer for her afternoon naps, went off. She pulled on a sunny yellow dress with blue trim — one of his favorites.

Be a little gay and a little more interesting for him.

She pinched her cheeks to add color and removed the scarf and curlers. Her hair hadn't gotten wet in the ocean or the shower. The shock from the winter-chilled water sucked the air from her lungs when it hit her chest, turning a switch back on in her brain, forcing her legs and arms to turn her around and march her back to shore. She almost looked pretty after brushing and setting her hair. The lack of flush to her face made her green eyes glow.

She broke her gaze to review the magazine that had arrived for him, readying herself for conversation.

Clear away the clutter.

She tiptoed by the closed bedroom door and the unused bathroom where her clothes hung to drip dry. Her eyes focused on the plush carpet of the hallway, then made her way to prepare for the evening. The magazine placed just so next to his chair. The coaster set perfectly out of range of his elbow or gesturing hand.

Gather up schoolbooks, toys, papers, etc., and then run a dustcloth over the tables.

The library book on plumbing, with a letter from a certain friend sharing news of her latest pregnancy tucked between the pages, shut up inside a drawer. The wrench and bucket hidden under the sink in case her repair didn't hold. A fresh sweep of the kitchen and a run of the carpet sweeper around the living room erased every speck of the day.

Over the cooler months of the year, you should prepare a fire for him to unwind by.

Her mother always referred to May as her biggest disappointment in moving to Wilda Point from New York City. Often damp and socked with fog. The mud-coated landscape grabbed at shoes and flecked the bottoms of skirts and pants' legs. Spring hadn't yet burst forth to offer hope. But her father was tired of the city and wanted to discover his inner wild man. He loved every minute. Her mother never stopped complaining.

She never minded the mud and the fog all that much. And readied the logs and kindling in the fireplace, touching the long-lit match to the newspaper under the logs. Her fingers held her hair back as she blew life into the embers.

Prepare the children.

She sat back on her heels, pulled the small stone from the dress pocket, and held it to her emptiness. She tried to envision Life as instructed, but all she saw were the flames.

Be happy to see him.

His tires crunched along the gravel road to the big house with the empty bedrooms — so many unopened doors. She greeted him as he walked into the kitchen. He kissed her soft cheek.

Greet him with a warm smile and show sincerity in your desire to please him.

She smiled.

Listen to him.

And tilted her head.

Make the evening his.

He sniffed the fragrance from her neck. The one that shop girl suggested on the trip they took years ago, hurrying to drink in life before they settled into their dream.

Your goal: Try to make sure your home is a place of peace, order, and tranquility where your husband can renew himself in body and spirit.

She turned on the radio.

Don't greet him with complaints or problems.

He settled into his chair, then leaned back to review the mail. She excused herself to check on dinner and snuck a peak under the sink.

Don't complain if he's late for dinner or even if he stays out all night.

He called from the other room to say how good the dinner smelled and that he was starving. He was always home on time. Reliable. Eager.

Make him comfortable.

She poured Scotch into a glass and placed it on his coaster. Then removed his muddy shoes that rested on the ottoman and clapped them outside the kitchen door in the sharp evening air.

Don't ask him questions about his actions or question his judgment or integrity.

They relaxed into dinner. He made a big show out of every bite. The stone sat heavy in her pocket. With his mouth stuffed, he scanned the baren chairs around the table, his posture bent. The smile dropped from his face. He swallowed, lifted his shoulders, and recounted the office gossip over the new secretary's skirt.

A good wife knows her place.

After dinner, she lifted the stopper to one of the jars on the bookshelf and dropped her stone in. Altogether, the jars held a thousand small lucky stones gathered each day since they started trying for a family. Each a wish to fill the growing void.

He flopped the magazine over his leg, sighed, and reached for her hand. He told her how cute she was and how lucky they were to have everything they wanted.

How We Learned to Fly

Anita Hunt

Goldilocks Zone 2024 Winner

As storms move branches,
as a river pushes past fish in spawn,
we dance an eddy, a tight corner,
a swing of sky,
feet stepping across streams
on the backs of stones singing ancient melodies
only our bodies can hear.

We sit cross-legged on the ground until our spines are stone,
and rise as green stalks.
If bones were wood we'd stand for years, bending,
shedding a branch, a ragged twig,
to come into balance, stronger at the break,
roots tangling with older bones
hardened in the frost.

We vine through branches, roof-lines;
fledgling coils reach higher each year, pursuing flight
above abandoned nests
and the shelter of walls.

The last elm has died.
Its skeleton turns silver,
magnificent and smooth as stones buried at sea.
Limbs feed our fires, which feed us, sending
smoke, invasive as knapweed, into the still air.

Argestes, In Heat

Paloma Maria Freitas

Solar Flare 2024 Finalist

The wind kept Maya from leaving the bed.

It was the fear of the wind which interfered with her leaving the arms of her lover and flying home to her own bed, where she'd much rather be.

It wasn't exactly a fear of the wind that plagued her, but a fear of the sound it made. Not every sound it made. Not whistling through pressed-layer canyons or flittering through the silvery leaves of bay trees. Even the gales of a hurricane side streaked with rain. These were fine sounds, beautiful sounds, calming, peaceful sounds that meant the world was turning as it should. It was only the winds which sparked change that terrified Maya, the winds that signaled a shift in the weather, the ones which ignited disaster.

Maya had been 19 years old when the winds pounded against her bedroom window and the thin wooden walls and the metal roof of the house where she lived. But the sleepless night she endured as branches collapsed from their limbs and limbs from their trees beyond the walls of her home that shook when the thunder came each May would not be the origin of her terror.

There was yard work to be done the next morning, hours of cleaning up the wooded area surrounding her home. Branches as long as she was and twice as heavy required strategizing; they could not be so easily taken care of with a rake or a weed-whacker in the ways of normal chores which were always tedious, but thankfully, also thoughtless.

Alexander's naked body pushed up against her from behind — in what Maya hoped was an act entranced in a deep sleep. If there was a chance of leaving, she knew it must be now. That would mean facing the wind. The wind, like Alexander, had never hurt Maya directly. And like the wind, Alexander rarely caused Maya any sort of distress. But then the wind would whip in such a way, and he would blow by, having missed her, needing to hold her.

His grasp was strong. There would be storms of purple and pea-soup-green clouds of bruising across her curves when Maya looked down at herself in the shower. But she wasn't in danger. Unlike the wind, he could protect her. He had strong arms he would wrap around Maya. He would pull her to his chest to let her know what he wanted. Those arms could keep the wind away. If he was holding her, if he was touching her, if he was inside her, she wasn't alone with the sounds of air moving.

That was all it was. Maya knew that's all it was. And now, far away and free from the crackling summers where she'd grown up, she could remind and reassure herself that wind frequently brought rain as well. Cool, extinguishing rain to keep grass from browning and tree bark from brittling.

As a child she had loved the crunching sound and soft pricking pain of the dead grass beneath her bare feet as she picked bark off the trees in large puzzle pieces with the lightest of touches. She'd create beautiful patterns of deep browns and tans and ashen grays at the height of a seven-year-old across every elm in her yard. As she grew older, the game became a habit. One that caught light and spread into her neighborhood as she was allowed to venture out further on her own. And it was always alone.

Maya did not mind being alone then, and she now preferred it. At least most of the time. When the wind was gone, there was no reason to want anyone over, even Alexander. Though, she did like him. She liked him much more than anyone else who might come over. And if he was there, Maya could curl up inside him, safety hidden from the wind. He would serve as her protector. There would still be the noise, but that was easily drowned out with the rest of her thoughts, washed away, extinguished by louder sounds and fiercer touches.

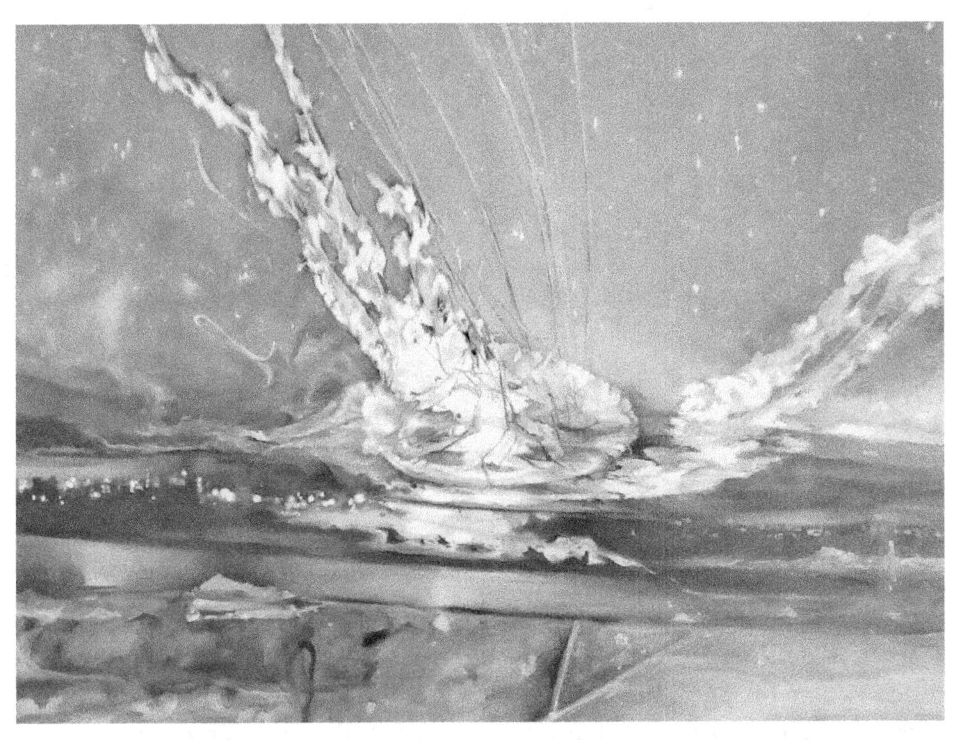

Impact / Katie Wilde

Solar Flare 2024 Finalist

The Banger

Rebecca Winterer

Solar Flare 2024 Finalist

It started when George hit her hand. Pickleballs sting. And surprise when they strike you hard from across the net. A drive aimed perfectly. She pretended it didn't sting, though she did shake and wriggle her fingers some. "Good shot," she said. But, was it? Good if he'd meant to throw her into a netherworld of smarting defense. George was tall with long muscular arms. Good too to remind her to wear her protective eyewear forgotten on the kitchen counter. He'd shown Mandy that she hadn't been prepared: her shot high, her paddle slow and low. Now a face hit was not only possible, but probable. She'd practically encouraged him by saying "good shot" like that, like do more of those. Effective strategy, George.

She and her partner, Tim, lost two points while she deliberated on the hit. Tim cleared his throat and although he didn't say "Hello, Mandy, it's lonely playing alone here," she knew the throat thing said as much. "And bangers bang," he added, under his breath, which was kind and a little funny since Tim's game could be equally strident.

Their point and it was now Tim's serve. George returned it with a forehand drive to Mandy, which she drove back to him and he to her, each moving incrementally forward. She didn't want to acknowledge she was wary moving forward. The closer to the net, the more extreme the impact, yet the further and longer she stayed back the more she disadvantaged she and Tim. Tim and George's partner June had already moved up to the non-volley-zone yet Mandy and George ignored them, locked into a peculiar one-sided volley hands battle from midcourt. This isn't how to play pickleball well. George had to be thinking the same.

Mostly Mandy, it's not a good idea to reflect on non-pickleball moments in the heat of a point or anytime during a match.

It was a great party. It was a wake, Mandy. Jimmy, her brother, was always judgy. They'd hauled their mother's Lenox dishes into her back yard, a weedy lot overlaid with cement. It was the Butterfly Meadow Monarch dinnerware set and they'd hated the flowers, bugs, scalloped edges, the "every meal is springtime" comment when their mother dumped takeout over those coy blossoms and wings. They stood on foldable chairs and smashed one dish after another onto the concrete: a bang, bang, bang cacophony of broken colored pottery. Wasted as their mother on a sober day.

George's volleys came harder. Her returns more reactive now. She'd never ducked at home. It infuriated Jimmy. "Pure idiocy to be punched by a blind-drunk, Mandy, but the eldest knows best, right!" George's face red and shining. It's weird what you miss. How a child will, no matter what, long for their mother. George's returns were creeping higher, head level. She knew that she could easily duck and let the pickleball fly out.

Midday Living / Drie Chapek

Solar Flare 2024 Finalist

Goddess Musings #1

Micaela Foreman

Solar Flare 2024 Finalist

I've begun to see strange faces look back up at me when I kneel down at the riverbed to pray. Faces that aren't quite mine. Faces that are very mine. Faces that I own but cannot wear. Water rippling across features that I had only seen in forgotten dreams. Sometimes it makes my skin itch. Makes me question whether this skin can be shed like a tarantula molts. I wonder if there is anything underneath. Or if all this body can be is blood and meat and memory.

The sun is setting. I've lost track of time again. It feels like counting grains of sand. Moving one grain from a pile sitting on my right to a pile sitting on my left. And just when the pile on my left grows to be as tall as I am, I forget what number I was on and I am cursed to start over. And another year of my human life has passed. I am sure *God* could hold all my grains of rice in the palm of *Her* heavy, wrinkled hand. Did you know there are metric tons of water tucked away into dainty clouds? I imagine there are trillions of raindrops wrapped into hurricanes, I bet *God* has had to count those too. I wonder if an eternal life can be wasted.

I don't have to worry about a wasted life. The water living in the sky has known centuries more than my body ever will. The clouds so much more expansive than my flesh can ever willingly allow me to feel. I wonder if the clouds ever felt the need to be smaller. To be controlled by some sky wizard who gets fed cattle and choir boys. I wonder if *God* has ever wanted to bathe in the blood of sacrifice and have raw sex on the altar. I wonder if *She* ever wished *She* had another all-knowing being that controlled *Her*. Something to dissolve into, to relinquish the heavy agency of a body that was never meant to be. A body that could not maintain its tenuous constitution, constantly tempted by the need to be all but doomed by the call to be one.

My grandmother once said that eons ago, *She* watched herself explode into the heat of the expanding universe. Ever since *She* has traveled through space and time trying to find *Her* missing pieces. I can taste *Her* longing in the raindrops I keep mistaking for my own tears when they trace the outline of my face. Perhaps, these are *Her* faces I see here, reflected back to me. I imagine the rain hears her plea to be reunited, so it collects the found faces before returning to the river and emptying back out from the delta into the ocean. I hope one day, *She* finds me too.

A Lost Coastline / Dylan James Seeman

Solar Flare 2024 Best of Art

THE HAPPY SON

JR FENN

SOLAR FLARE 2024 WINNER

I stood in the rain. My father came and looked at me, there in the front yard. Your eyes are bright, he said. Thank you, I said. You may have them. He put them in his jewel box, locked the box with the key he wore at his neck, tucked the key back under his shirt. After this he'd hum and chop the onions and laugh at the tears that sprang into his eyes. I could see it all clearly with the sight of the spirit. I ran and jumped over the line where the kitchen became the pantry, my hair a blaze down my back. In the silence, I turned. Your hair, he said. You may have it, I said. Please, it is yours. And he took my hair as I bent my head, the sting of water where my eyes had been as the knife sawed, soft as could be. After this he put on his work shorts and tended the vines and gathered the peaches from the tree. Look, he said, what bounty is before us. And the land stretched as far as the eye could see in all its goodness, the two of us resting after the harvest, our legs bare and warming in the heat. They are beautiful, my father said. And they were — my legs, brown and long as a boychild's legs become when he has grown taller. And there in the sun on the red picnic blanket, all the world rising in its splendid orchestra of cicadas and birds and streams and cirrus clouds that flitted high above in the celestial orb, I paused, and said, You may have them. Though my heart leapt in my throat. You may have them, I said, for you are the one who gave me life. And my father took them as gently as the grapes from the vines, and put them in the box, and we made pegs for me to stand and walk with my sheared head, and to marvel at penumbras with my spiritual sight. That night I heard a noise in the room with the box. I went to the door. I saw, on the far side of the room, my father wrapped in a glorious light. He was small as a child, with eyes of emerald and a cloud of boy hair and long legs that led down as if all the way back to childhood. On the floor I saw something dark, and a glint: my father's shirt, and the key. I picked them up. My father turned. I couldn't see his face, the window silhouetting him from behind. But I could see him move toward me with a round, tripping gait, in the manner of all those who are newly born, and trying to live, and to walk and be free. And when he came closer, when I saw his joyful, weeping face, I wondered at what I had given — for he was the son, and I was the father.

GLIMPSE OF PARADISE / GERBURG GARMANN

STEP INTO MY GARDEN / GERBURG GARMANN

Bauhaus Los Angeles / Holly Willis

AI Assisted

Heroes and Villains Enhanced

/ GJ Gillespie

AI Assisted

FOREVER YOUNG ENHANCED / GJ GILLESPIE

AI ASSISTED

WAITING ROOM / TANDEM TANGENTS

AI ASSISTED

Augmentiquities, Ersatz Ecologies

/ Caleb Weintraub

AI Assisted

Souvenirs from the Uncanny Valley / Caleb Weintraub

AI Assisted

Infinite Inspiration / Gerburg Garmann

AI Assisted

CONTRIBUTORS

Jack Bordnick's sculptures and photography incorporate surrealistic, mythological and magical imagery often with whimsical overtones – aimed at provoking our experiences and self-reflections. Aiming to unbalance our rational minds, the predominant imagery deals mostly with facial expressions of both living and "non-living" beings, and things that speak to us in their own languages. They are mixed media assemblages that have been assembled, disassembled and reassembled, becoming abstractions unto themselves. Enjoy their stories.

Aimee Bungard is an artist living and working in the hills of Appalachia just outside Pittsburgh with her guitar player husband, 3 freerange children, 2 Suessian mutts and 1 perfect Torti kitty. She considers Giacometti, Vincent, Frida, Hilma Af Klint, Tascha Tudor, Bukowski, Dylan, Townes Van Zandt and RamDass to be of the highest inspiration.

Kristian Butterfield is a poet from Tampa, FL. He holds a BA in Creative Writing from Florida State University. Kristian's work appears previously in *Book of Matches, Door is a Jar, The Owl Research Magazine*, and elsewhere. He currently lives in Chicago, IL where he works in investments.

Anita Cabrera's poetry, creative nonfiction, and fiction have appeared in *The New Guard, Acentos Review, Anti-Heroin Chic, Litro Magazine, Berkeley Fiction Review, The Best Women's Travel Writing, Volume 12, Deronda*, and other journals. Her work has been nominated for a Pushcart Award and adapted for stage by the Bay Area Word for Word Theater Company.

J Carraher is a writer based in the San Francisco Bay Area. Her work has appeared in such venues as *The Open Window, Severance Magazine, The University of California of Press, Sunspot Literary Journal* and *Memoir Ink*. When she is not writing, J makes her living as a forensic examiner and lecturer. She is also a reviewer for Elsevier.

Aaron Carrot leads a double life; by day a city project manager, by night a household member. He writes on the subway, shuttling between these disparate worlds. Fortunately his commute is a long one and affords ample opportunity to dream.

Drie Chapek constructs her painted environments with personal reminders of complexity, pain, pleasure and delight discovered within these worlds. Prepared as a visual reminder of embracing emotional health to live in the present Through the breath and somatic experiencing Chapek is able to hold the variables of life so that she can stay in her body as an active participant of her human experience.

Composing collisions of energies gives Chapek a visual field in which to explore and connect her life's joy and grief experiences.

Annie Dawid's photographs have appeared on the covers of *Into the Void*, *Cake*, *Blue Earth Review*, *The Westchester Review*, *Oregon Focus* and *American Poetry Review*; and her assemblages have been featured in multiple art shows in Colorado.

Emily Dolanová has enjoyed writing and drawing through her many adventures, including being a professional horseback rider, living in a van and running a homestead. An English teacher by trade, she is currently located in the Czech Republic with her dog and parrots.

JR Fenn's work has appeared in *Boston Review*, *Gulf Coast*, *DIAGRAM*, Versal, and *PANK*, among other places. Fenn holds an MFA in Fiction from Syracuse University, where she won the Joyce Carol Oates Prize in Fiction. She lives with her family in western New York.

Kathy Flann is the author of four books. A humor book, *How to Survive a Human Attack: A Guide for Werewolves, Mummies, Cyborgs, Ghosts, Nuclear Mutants, and Other Movie Monsters* was released by Running Press (Hachette). A short story collection, *Smoky Ordinary*, won the Serena McDonald Kennedy Award and was published by Snake Nation Press. A collection of short stories, *Get a Grip*, recipient of the George Garrett Fiction Prize, was published by the Texas Review Press. My craft book, *Write On: Secrets to Crafting Better Stories*, was released in 2021 by Stay Thirsty Media. Kathleen grew up in Virginia, and received an MFA from UNC-Greensboro. For five years, she taught creative writing at the University of Cumbria in England, where she created mini-courses for the BBC's Get Writing website and served on the board of the National Association of Writers in Education. Currently, she teaches fiction writing in the MA program at Johns Hopkins University.

Adrian Fleur is a writer based in Minneapolis, United States, but she's previously lived in Thailand, Spain, and the United Kingdom. Her novel *Zithande* is based in the Eastern Cape of her home country South Africa, and explores the power of women's friendship across class and racial lines, collective resilience in the face of grief, and the deliberate act of seeking joy. You can find out more about her at www.adrianfleur.com.

Micaela Foreman is an astrophysicist who tries to find time to contemplate the vastness of the universe between her grad school classes.

Sculptures by US-based **Irwin Freeman** have exhibited at museums in Phoenix, Hattiesburg, Providence.

Paloma Maria Freitas is an American writer and theatre-maker currently based in the UK. She received a BFA in creative writing from Southern Oregon University. Her short fiction and poetry has been published by *Midway Journal* and *Messy Misfits Club*. Additionally, her short play *Delights* was performed in North London in 2023.

Gerburg Garmann, a painter, poet, and recently retired professor of Global Languages and Cross-Cultural Studies at the University of Indianapolis, USA, is now fully concentrating on the arts. Her scholarly publications appear in English, German, and French in international journals. Her artwork and poems have appeared in various magazines and anthologies around the world. She specializes in creating art for women. For more information, please visit her website www.gerburggarmann.com.

GJ Gillespie is a collage artist living in a 1928 farmhouse overlooking Oak Harbor on Whidbey Island, WA. A prolific artist with 20 awards to his name, his work has been exhibited in 64 shows and appeared in more than 140 publications. Beyond his studio practice, Gillespie channels his passion for art by running Leda Art Supply, a company specializing in premium sketchbooks. Whether conjuring vivid collage compositions or enabling other artists through exceptional tools, Gillespie remains dedicated to the transformative power of art.

Robert Gillespie is a multidisciplinary artist from Derry, Northern Ireland, now living and working in London. He grew up during the Troubles and investigates themes of cognitive dissonance and belief systems through multiple series of paintings, conceptual photography, and other media.

Chad Gusler has an MFA in fiction, an MA in religious studies, and a BS in theology. His stories have been published in *Broad River Review*, *Driftwood*, *Southwest Review*, *The Maine Review*, and elsewhere. His works have been finalists for the Calvino Award, the Ron Rash Award in Fiction, and the Tobias Wolff Award in Fiction. He teaches at Eastern Mennonite University in Harrisonburg, Virginia.

Milo Harvey is a visual artist based in Los Angeles with concentrations in photography, sculpture and poetry. Harvey's work explores transgender and queer identity, sexual trauma, childhood trauma, transitioning and gender norms through a heavy focus on the body and self.

JC Chen Henderson publishes fiction, poetry, and visual art in literary reviews and poetry magazines. Her work appears in journals such as *Fourteen Hills*, *Poetry East*, *Sunspot Literary Journal*, *Freshwater Review*, *The Pointed Circle*, *The Clackamas Review*, and *SLANT*, to name a few. Henderson strives to express spirituality and sexuality in her work. She has sold hundreds of her paintings.

Indyana Horobin is a PhD candidate studying at Griffith, with major focusses in modern history and creative writing. He has had a publication in Drunken Boat's 2020 anthology *Meridian*, and a short story published in APWT's *Pratik: Fire and Rain*. His current PhD project focusses on familial oral histories told in memoir.

Anita Hunt is a poet and retired adjunct professor from Cadillac, Michigan, who writes about her experiences living in rural northern Michigan and southwestern Montana. She holds an MA in Humanities from Central Michigan University, and a BA in Writing from Denison University. Anita is the recipient of the 2023 ArtFest 55 first place award for poetry. Her work has appeared in the *Montana Poet*, *The Feast* (Episcopal,) and the *Oprelle/Matter* anthology.

Leslie Kerby's art is held at Columbia University, Arkansas State University, Copelouzos Art Museum, Greece. Art commissions from Norte Maar Gallery, BRIC Arts | Media and Visual Arts Center of New Jersey. Residencies include Virginia Center for Creative Arts Virginia and France, the American Academy in Rome and School of Visual Arts.

G.R. Kramer grew up in Canada, Kenya, and the U.S., the child of refugees from fascism and communism. His first poetry chapbook was published by Finish Line Press in 2023. Other places where his poems appear include the *Atlanta Review*, *Mudfish*, *The New York Times*, and *The Winter Anthology*.

Emily Krill is an artist and graphic designer living in Pittsburgh. She makes collages out of paper ephemera, like ledger books from the 1800s, spelling homework from the 1940s, and mimeographs from the 1970s. It's all mixed up in bright and colorful ways. Emily's main concern is that her work makes people happy. She thinks art should be like the City of Pittsburgh: livable.

Robb Kunz hails from Teton Valley, Idaho. He received his MFA in creative writing from the University of Idaho. He currently teaches writing at Utah State University and is the Art and Design Faculty Advisor of *Sink Hollow: An Undergraduate Literary Journal*. His art has been published in *Peatsmoke Journal*, *Red Ogre Review*, *Fatal Flaw Literary Magazine*, and *New Delta Review*. His art is upcoming in *Ponder Review*, *Glassworks Magazine*, and *Anodyne Magazine*.

David Landau is an alumnus of the Iowa Writers' Workshop summer program. His story *Sweetheart* was shortlisted for the Aesthetica Creative Writing Award and is published in their 2024 Award Anthology. Another story made the New Writing Prize longlist from *Wasafiri*, the UK's leading magazine for international contemporary writing. Other works can be read in *The Cossack Review*, *580 Split*, and *Write City Magazine*.

Rosa Lane is author of four poetry collections including *Called Back* (forthcoming, Tupelo Press); *Chouteau's Chalk* (2019, UGA Poetry Prize); *Tiller North* (2016, Sixteen Rivers); and *Roots and Reckonings* (chapbook). She won the 2023 Morton Marcus Memorial Poetry Prize and has appeared in *Asheville Poetry Review, Massachusetts Review, RHINO*, and elsewhere.

Kyo Lee is a Korean-Canadian high school student. She is the youngest winner of the CBC Poetry Prize and finalist for the RBC Bronwen Wallace Award. You can find her in *PRISM, Nimrod, Synergy, This Magazine* and others. Her debut poetry collection will be published in 2025. She loves summer storms.

Anita Maksimiuk is currently an MFA student living and working in Tucson, Arizona. Born and raised in Brooklyn, NY, she is constantly inspired by her home city, as well as her adopted one. Anita is a writer and printmaker working in screen print and traditional stone lithography. Photography and travel are a huge part of her printmaking practice, as each piece begins with a photo from her personal archive. Passions include writing, languages, music, and adventure by way of endurance.

Caitlyn Moony is a South African-Canadian writer living in Vancouver, Canada. She enjoys travelling the world and writing about the various oddballs that scuttle about inside her head.

Pablo Neruda (born July 12, 1904, Parral, Chile — died September 23, 1973, Santiago) was a Chilean poet, diplomat, and politician who was awarded the Nobel Prize for Literature in 1971. He is perhaps the most important Latin American poet of the 20th century.

Jordan Nishkian is an Armenian-Portuguese writer based in California. Her prose and poetry explore themes of duality and have been featured in national and international publications. She has been awarded the Rollick Magazine Fiction Prize and has been nominated for the Pushcart Prize and Best American Short Stories. Jordan is the Editor-in-Chief of *Mythos* literary magazine and the author of *Kindred*, a novella.

Michael Noonan comes from Halifax (home of the Piece Hall), West Yorkshire. He has a background in retail, food production and office work. He has had artworks published in literary journals in the US, UK, and internationally, including *After the Pause, Utopia Science Fiction Magazine, Noctivigant Press, Baby Teeth Journal, Odd Magazine, Wild Roof Journal, Press Pause Press, Indicia, Hooghly Review, Last Leaves Magazine, Collidescope, Thimble Lit Mag, Does it have Pockets, The Concrete Desert Review, 805 Lit+Art!, Qwerty, Suspended Magazine, Full House Literary Magazine*, and *Spellbinder*, literary and arts quarterly. He won a runner-up prize for a black-and-white line

drawing in a competition run by *Arts and Illustrators Magazine* in the UK. His drawings, *The Pedestrian Centre*, and *Fun Girl*, for which he has been awarded certificates, were shown at the CityScapes and Figurative art exhibitions, run by the Light, Space and Time online art gallery in America; and can be seen on their youtube videos. His own painting can be seen on the cover of a volume of his short stories, entitled, *Seven Tall Tales*, that is available at Amazon. He admires the great surrealist artists like Rene Magritte, Max Ernst, and Chirico; and his particular favourite is Yves Tanguy. He likes the subversive and the dreamlike quality of their work, and many of his own artworks have a tendency towards the offbeat and the unusual. Michael's online art portfolio is:
https://www.behance.net/gallery/182795873/Imaginative-Images

In Toronto, **Leah Oates** has had a solo show at Black Cat Artspace and group shows at the Gladstone Hotel, John. B. Aird Gallery, Gallery 1313, Propeller Gallery, Remote Gallery, Arta Gallery, and at the Papermill Gallery. She's had solo shows at venues such as Susan Eley Fine Art, The Arsenal Gallery in Central Park, The Brooklyn Public Library, The Center for Book Arts, Tomasulo Gallery, Real Art Ways, and at the Sol Mednick Gallery at the Philadelphia University of the Arts and national and international solo shows at Anchor Graphics, Artemisia Gallery and Woman Made Gallery in Chicago, Illinois and at Galerie Joella in Turku, Finland. The series in this issue was featured from 2016-2017 as part of the MTA Arts and Design Light Box Project at 42nd Street in New York City. Leah's work has been in group shows in the NYC area at the Schweinfurth Art Center, Brooklyn's Prospect Park, Nurture Art Gallery, Metaphor Projects , Denise Bibro Fine Art, The Pen and Brush Gallery and nationally at Bob Rauschenberg Gallery in Florida, Unsettled Gallery in New Mexico, A Smith Gallery in Texas, and at LICHTUNDFIRE Gallery in NYC.

Christy O'Callaghan is a dyslexic writer and developmental editor in Upstate, NY. She has spent a quarter of a century as a community organizer and educator. Christy loves strange stories, plants, and lore. Her work has appeared in *The Los Angeles Review*, *Great Weather for Media*, *Trolley Journal*, *Under the Gumtree*, *Chestnut Review*, and more. christyflutterby.com

Stephen Policoff's first novel, *Beautiful Somewhere Else*, won the James Jones Award, and was published by Carroll & Graf in 2004. His 2nd novel, *Come Away*, won the Dzanc Award, and was published by Dzanc Books in 2014. His 3rd novel, *Dangerous Blues*, was published by Flexible Press in 2022. He is Clinical Professor of Writing in Global Liberal Studies at NYU.

René Karl Wilhelm Johann Josef Maria Rilke (4 December 1875 — 29 December 1926), better known as **Rainer Maria Rilke**, was an Austrian poet and novelist. Rilke is appreciated as one of the most lyrical German-language poets. He wrote one novel in lyrical prose, *The Notebooks of Malte Laurids Brigge* (*Die Aufzeichnungen des Malte Laurids Brigge*), but mostly wrote verse, although he is also known for several collections of his voluminous correspondence. Rilke's work is often considered to be mystical, and his imagery often focuses on the challenge of being in communion with the ineffable – especially in what W. H. Auden termed "the age of anxiety." Rilke is also known for his contributions to French literature for his having written over 400 poems, originally written in French, and dedicated to the canton of Valais, in Switzerland. However, he is more renowned for his collections of poetry, written toward the end of his life, *Duino Elegies* (*Duineser Elegien*) and *Sonnets to Orpheus* (*Die Sonette an Orpheus*), as well as the posthumously collected *Letters to a Young Poet* (*Briefe an einen jungen Dichter*). In the early 20th century, a century after his death, Rilke is still one of the more popular and best-selling poets, whose work is also qualitatively and distinctly accomplished. He is also known for having chosen a poem he wrote for his epitaph, which bears a motif that can be found throughout his work, and that being the image of the rose, in all its variations. The poem on his gravestone in the churchyard of Raron, Switzerland reads: Rose, oh reiner Widerspruch, Lust, Niemandes Schlaf zu sein unter soviel Lidern. – Rainer Maria Rilke; Rose, o pure contradiction, desire To be the sleep that no one wants Under so many lids (Translator's Biographical Note)

Aleksandra Scepanovic's tumultuous journey toward sculpture began in socialist Yugoslavia in the 1980s. Shaping her voice and perspective was a list of varied career trajectories, which deposited her to archaeological sites, war zones of the Balkan conflicts in the 1990s, and interior design and real estate fields in New York City at the onset of the 2000s. Today, snippets from her past inspire Aleksandra's artistic spirit as she collaborates with a collective of sculptors in her studio in Woodstock, NY (@atelierwdstk_hudsonvalley). Through her art, Aleksandra celebrates the bravery of continuation, the joy of new explorations, and the thrill of a quiet life in the tranquil Hudson Valley. www.aleksandrasculpture.com

Dylan James Seeman, 29, born and raised in Phoenix, AZ. Self-taught, he began painting four years ago with extreme passion. Dylan's work centers around methodically heightening life's nostalgic moments to their limits.

Jennifer Seigle is a director-choreographer and writer who currently resides in Arizona. She published her first poem at the age of 14 and has been processing the world through words and movement ever since.

Almost entirely self-taught, **Heather P. Shreve** has been painting and selling her art since age eleven. Her first inspirations were wildlife and the simplicity of Sumi-e Japanese ink paintings. She is also an award-winning screenwriter, historian, author of six books, lives in Maryland, and has two children.

Dave Sims continues to make art and music in the old mountains of central Pennsylvania. See more at www.tincansims.com.

Alan Sincic is a teacher at Valencia College. His fiction has appeared in *Boulevard, New Ohio Review, The Greensboro Review, The Saturday Evening Post, Hunger Mountain, Big Fiction Magazine, A-3 Press, The Gateway Review, Cobalt,* and elsewhere. His short stories havee recently won contests sponsored by *The Texas Observer, Driftwood Press, The Prism Review, Westchester Review, American Writer's Review, Vincent Brothers Review, Pulp Literature,* and *Broad River Review.* After an MA in Lit at the University of Florida and a poetry fellowship at Columbia, Alan earned his MFA at Western New England University. Alan spent over a dozen years in NYC as a writer and performer — comic/satirical pieces that eventually became a pair of full-length plays (*American Obsessions* and *Breaking Glass*) at the Orlando International Fringe Festival.

Leah Skay received her BA in Writing from Ithaca College. She is a proud alumna of the Japanese Exchange and Teaching Program and has returned stateside with a renewed vigor for creating her award-winning fiction, nonfiction, and poetry (a new adventure).

Jackson Mills Smith is a poetry MFA candidate at the University of Montana who writes about the regional folklore, history, and natural landscape of his childhood home in rural Southwestern Indiana. Smith's work appears in *Making Waves: A West Michigan Review, The Quarter(ly), Wild Roof Journal,* and *Write Place.*

Joannie Stangeland is the author of several collections, most recently *The Scene You See* (Ravenna Press). Her poems have also appeared in *The Pedestal Magazine, New England Review, Prairie Schooner,* and other journals. Joannie holds an MFA from the Rainier Writing Workshop.

Lenora Steele's poetry and short prose has been published or accepted for publication in: *Atlanta Review, Event, The Fiddlehead, The New Quarterly, Eastern Iowa Review, The Fourth River,* and others. She lives where the dykes hold back the muddy red waters of Bay of Fundy in Truro, Nova Scotia, Canada.

Wally Swist's books include *Huang Po and the Dimensions of Love* (Southern Illinois University Press, 2012), selected by Yusef Komunyakaa for the 2011 Crab Orchard Open Poetry Competition, and *A Bird Who Seems to Know Me: Poems Regarding Birds and Nature*, winner of the 2018 Ex Ophidia Poetry Prize. Recent essays, poems, and translations have appeared in *Asymptote* (Taiwan), *Chicago Quarterly Review, Commonweal, The Comstock Review, Healing Muse: Center for Bioethics & Humanities, Illuminations, La Piccioletta Barca* (U.K.), *Pensive: A Journal of Global Spirituality, Tipton Poetry Review, Poetry London,* and *Your Impossible Voice.* Shanti Arts published his translation of *L'Allegria*, Giuseppe Ungaretti's first iconic book, in 2023. Swist will be a featured writer in the Spring 2025 issue of *Ezra: An Online Journal of Translation* that will highlight several of his translations from the Spanish of Roberto Juarroz. Forthcoming titles include three books of translation, one from Finishing Line Press, *If You're the Dreamer, I'm the Dream: Selected Translations from The Book of Hours*, and two from Pierian Springs Press, *A Sense of Order in the Disorder of the World: Selected Translations from the Spanish and Untranslatable Song: A Selection from the Vertical Poetry of Roberto Juarroz*, in 2025. Finishing Line Press will additionally be publishing a collection of Swist's "angel poems and translations," entitled *Of Angels*, in 2025.

As a dynamic artist duo, **Tandem Tangents** is a collaborative team formed by **Anduriel Widmark** and **Reece Salinas.** Blending distinct yet complementary skills, they create innovative artworks that straddle traditional and digital realms. With a foundation in classical art techniques, they integrate their traditional artwork into generative models to discover new perspectives and create interesting artifacts. Working together on every piece, they engage in a back-and-forth process of creative explorations. Sometimes they have a specific plan, while other times it's spontaneous, but their main focus is on having fun while creating together. Their collaborative pieces are a testament to their shared vision of pushing artistic boundaries and exploring new technological and expressive possibilities. Together, they continuously seek to grow, understand, be kind, and expand what's possible in the world.

Austin-based artist **Anna Troxell** cannot decide on a medium. Constantly torn, she embraces a mixed media approach. However, the study of the female body and how it is both adored and disposed of remains the focus. At times, the body is printed on fabric, sculpted, sewn and stuffed. Other explorations result in edible images, printed on rice paper and consumed in performance. She received her BFA in Photography from Tyler School of Art, and her MFA in Photography and Electronic Art from Maryland Institute College of Art. In addition, she remains committed to creative writing, which informs the visual work.

Garth Upshaw lives in Portland, Oregon, with his super-genius wife, three precocious grown children, and six enthusiastic chickens. His work has appeared in *Clarkesworld Magazine*, *Beneath Ceaseless Skies*, *Bristol Noir*, and other fine venues. He has an MA in Theoretical Mathematics and loves carving spoons, bicycling, and curling up with a good book.

Pamela Viggiani is a mixed-media artist and art educator living in Canandaigua, NY. A native of the Finger Lakes region, Pamela received a BS and MS from Nazareth College of Rochester. She began teaching art in 1986 and continues to foster enthusiasm and creativity in her students to this day.

Caleb Weintraub has exhibited nationally and internationally. Two of his paintings are featured in the book, *Signs of the Apocalypse/Rapture* published by Front Forty press, distributed by University of Chicago Press. A Feature article about his work was published in *Juxtapoz Magazine*. He has been an artist-in-residence at Redux Art Center in South Carolina and the Santa Fe Art Institute. Significant group shows include exhibitions at the Chicago Cultural Center, the Hyde Park Art Center, and Scion Art Space in Los Angeles. In 2019, Weintraub was a Fellow at the Institute for Digital Arts and Humanities, Indiana University.

Alfie White (b. 2000) is a writer born, raised, and based in South London. Alfie's work explores the nuances and intricacies of the human condition and of everyday life, with a focus on moments of emotion and human intimacy which they find meaningful.

Katie Wilde is a Canadian visual artist with an affinity for nature, oddness and interactivity. She holds a Bachelor of Fine Arts from the University of Ottawa, and has exhibited in a variety of contexts, including galleries, a biochemistry lab, a crosswalk, and the surface of a public square.

Rex Wilder is an award-winning photographer and poet. He is the author of four books of poetry. His fifth, *Rare Fuel*, winners of the prestigious Donna Wolf-Palacio Poetry Prize, will appear soon. His latest volume is called *A Quiet Place to Land.*

Holly Willis is a hybrid artist/theorist working primarily in film, video, and still photography. Her work often examines the materiality of the image within a broader context of new materialist philosophy and the histories of experimental film, video, and photography with the goal to design encounters with media that spark an embodied sense of curiosity and wonder, alongside critical reflection about our relationship with the matter around us.

William Lewis Winston lives in Oakland, California, where he taught English and history for four decades, also publishing student writing in school literary journals and newspapers. His poems appear in *Bearing Witness* (Zephyr Press 2002), *Margie, Ink Pot, Comstock Review, Poet Lore, Essential* (Underground Writers Association 2022), *Close Up* (Orchard Lea Press 2022), *What Is All This Sweet Work?* (Vita Brevis Press Anthology IV 2022), *Sunspot Literary Journal*, and *Consequence*; and he received an International Merit Award from *Atlanta Review*. His short story *The Sound of Snow Not Falling* was featured in the Philadelphia InterAct Theatre's 2005-06 Writing Aloud series (Adrift), then published in *Litro* in 2023. He has looked through camera lenses and processed his own photographs since age ten. Up to now, his street photography, in distant lands, he has kept to himself.

Rebecca Winterer is the author of *The Singing Ship*, awarded the Del Sol Press 2016 First Novel Prize and selected as a finalist for the Black Lawrence Press 2016 Big Moose Prize. Her stories have been published by *Puerto del Sol* and *Identity Theory*, the latter nominated for Best Small Fictions 2024. Winterer has received fellowships at the Millay Colony, the Vermont Studio Center, Virginia Center for Creative Arts, and Yaddo, and holds an MFA from Warren Wilson College. She is at work on a second novel as well as a collection of flash fiction on pickleball.

Jane Wiseman (she/her), a transplanted southeasterner, splits her time between the Sandia Mountains of New Mexico and very urban south Minneapolis. Her poetry has appeared most recently in *Feral*, *Eclectica*, *SWWIM Everyday*, *NBR* (Zoetic Press), and other journals, with poems forthcoming in *Main Street Rag* and *Southern Poetry Review*.

Tianyagenv Yan lives in a difficult-to-define diaspora. She uses light clay to make mini-dolls and tells stories about the lived experiences of isolation, alienation, and being haunted by spiritual beings that are thorny to rationalize.

Cynthia Yatchman is a Seattle based artist and art instructor. She shows extensively in the Pacific Northwest. Past shows have included Seattle University, the Tacoma and Seattle Convention Centers and the Pacific Science Center. Her art is housed in numerous public and private collections.

Ronnie Yates has published poems and art reviews in *Colorado Review*, *Ploughshares*, *Quarter to Eight*, *Arts and Culture* (Houston) and on *Bomblog* and *Verse Daily*, and recently was a finalist for the Gigantic Sequins 12th Annual Flash Fiction Contest (forthcoming in June 2024). Ronnie is an educator, and most recently taught poetry and literature in the Texas Prison System through the University of Houston Clear Lake's Distance Learning Undergraduate and Graduate Degree Programs.

Based in Borrego Springs California, artist **Robin Young** works in mixed media focusing mostly on collage and contemporary art making. Her focus on collage art using magazine clippings, masking tape, wallpaper, jewelry, feathers, foil, etc., allows her to develop deep into the whimsical and intuitive. From large, life-sized pieces and 3D sculptures to small postcard-sized arrangements, Robin's keen eye and gripping esthetic guide her viewers into her own semi-readymade world.

Elizabeth Yuan is a senior from Adlai E. Stevenson High School in Illinois. She has previously been recognized by Scholastic Art & Writing awards. In her spare time, she enjoys falling down a rabbit hole of Wikipedia articles and drinking unhealthy amounts of coffee.

www.ingramcontent.com/pod-product-compliance
Lightning Source LLC
Chambersburg PA
CBHW070508200726
48293CB00007B/2447

* 9 7 8 1 9 5 1 3 8 9 3 7 6 *